HIKE for H...
SOUTHERN ...
Go-as-you-please ...
get you to the cou...
Ask for details at any S-...
'Southern Rambles' by ...

...OUT THIS BOOK

...North Devon railway line between
...er and Barnstaple runs for 39 miles
...n the River Exe to the Taw estuary
...ugh some of south-west England's
...liest countryside. From Eggesford
...rthward the route borders "the Country
...the Two Rivers" -- the home of Henry
...illiamson's Tarka the Otter.

The book you are now holding has evolved
over several years. It first saw the light of
day in April 2009 as a short booklet of 22
walks, all of them accessible by rail from
stations along the "Tarka Line". In this form,
the booklet was named by the Association
of Community Rail Partnerships as the U.K.'s
"Best Railway Marketing Publication" of
the year. Within weeks, there was pressure
for a second such booklet, and in April
2011 *More Tarka Line Walks*, featuring
a further batch of 22 self-guided hikes,
made its appearance. Fortunately, the
superb scenery effortlessly supported this
addition to the family, and once again all
walks were accessible by train.

In this book the 44 original walks, updated
where necessary, are for the first time
available in a single publication. In response
to many requests this volume features,
also for the first time, 16 additional walks
including several from the line's two *termini*,
Exeter St. David's and Barnstaple. All told,
the book offers the reader more than 325
miles of Devon footpaths and country lanes
to explore.

Like its predecessors, this book is intended
to encourage rea...ers -- whether regular
line users or leis...re trav...
train as a means of ex...
of the surroundi...g co...

leng...
shor...
the l...
day ... ...c...ience of public transport
and the satisfaction of leaving behind only
the most minimal of carbon footprints.

In these days of dire predictions about
rising obesity rates and associated health
problems, it's reassuring to know that
walking can do wonders for middle-age
spread (and, doubtless, other spreads!) But,
for those readers who have worked up a
well-deserved appetite, the location of local
pubs, tearooms (and shops) is given at the
beginning of every walk. Apart from sensible
footwear, raingear, this booklet and a train
timetable, no special equipment is needed.

The train timetable (FGW 34) is essential.

Some stations, indicated in this
book by the 🕐 symbol, have
only a very limited Monday to
Saturday service. Walks from
these remoter points fully
repay the effort of getting
there and back, but don't be stranded.
When planning your walk, please check
there's a train to take you home!

The countryside, which seems so tranquil from
the train window, is far from static. Village shops
and post offices, telephone boxes and footpaths
are all liable to change. Even Ordnance Survey
maps, reproduced in these pages by permission,
become less reliable with age and there are
a couple of occasions when the route shown
diverges from the footpath marked on the
OS map. While every ...ffort has been made
...the ...rmation in this book is
... m... more than a snapshot
...out... ...ated with time. To report

any inaccuracies, please use the author's e-mail address: pcbcraske@gmail.com

Where space allows, an effort has been made to offer some insight into the history of the railway, of the turnpike road that preceded it and of their combined impact upon the communities along the line.

HOW STRENUOUS?

Each walk has been graded into one of three levels of exertion, indicated by the number of boot symbols:

 Easy, and not too tiring for children.

 Moderate.

 Longer and more strenuous outings.

Every step has been walked by the author -- a pensioner who has known the line since the 1940s -- by his rescued labrador, Scrumpy, and by a motley assortment of middle-aged canine companions (who've enthusiastically covered at least triple the stated mileages!)

MUD, MUD, GLORIOUS MUD

Only on three or four walks in this series are you likely to encounter that Devon speciality: really severe mud (and in each case only for a few hundred yards). Depending on local rainfall, Morchard Road: Walk 1., Umberleigh: Walk 4. and Chapelton: Walk 3. each year compete for the coveted title of "Muddiest Tarka Line Walk". Wear high-sided waterproof boots, and you should encounter few problems but, when you see this ⬛ symbol, please consider yourself duly 🥾 warned!

HOW LONG?

Estimates about the time each walk will take are given only as a rough guide. Some will eschew pubs and take stiles and mud in their stride, intent on getting back to the station in time for the earliest train home, and determined to

complete all 60 walks in the space of a single summer. Others, more sensibly, will opt to take their time. Of this latter group, John Ruskin (1819-1900) would doubtless have approved.

"There was always more in the world than men could see, walked they ever so slowly; they will see it no better for going fast. The really precious things are thought and sight, not pace. It does ... a man ... no harm to go slow; for his glory is not at all in going, but in being."

Or, as the hand-painted sign at the entrance to a remote New England hamlet succinctly put it, "SLOW -- is fast enough."

MILES vs METRES

After nearly half a century the nation's on-again off-again relationship with the metric system continues unabated. In response to strongly expressed reader preference, distances in this book are given in old-fashioned and outdated yards and miles, longer distances are expressed in miles with a decimal point.

● **BARNSTAPLE**
● CHAPELTON
● UMBERLEIGH
● PORTSMOUTH ARMS
● KING'S NYMPTON
● EGGESFORD
● LAPFORD
● MORCHARD ROAD
● COPPLESTONE
● YEOFORD
● CREDITON
● NEWTON ST CYR
● **EXETER**

TARKA LINE

THE COUNTRYSIDE CODE

While the walks in this guide follow innumerable lanes, public footpaths, bridleways and other public rights of way, the fields they lead across are private and provide hardworking farmers with their living. Bearing in mind that the publication of this book will increase foot traffic across their land, please be respectful of farmers' property. In particular:

- Shut all gates.
- Keep dogs under close control, especially around livestock.
- Most, but not all, footpaths are clearly signed. Use the map. If you feel you've lost the path, retrace your steps.
- Do not leave litter. If a previous walker has done so, pick it up and take it home with you.
- Leave nothing behind . . . except footprints.

PHYSICAL IMPAIRMENTS

Unfortunately, the walks in this book are not suitable for individuals with physical impairments, requiring as they do an ability to negotiate stiles, muddy paths and steep ascents. Excellent alternative walking opportunies for people with physical impairments may be found, for example, at walkswithwheelchairs.com.

PHONE NUMBERS & NATIONAL RAIL ENQUIRIES

Timetables and fares information may be downloaded from www.firstgreatwestern. co.uk or obtained by calling National Rail Enquiries on 08457-484950. Pocket timetables can also be obtained from staffed stations.

ACKNOWLEDGEMENTS

This book would not have been possible without the generous support and encouragement of numerous organisations and individuals. Particular thanks are expressed to Sue Evans, Julian Crow MBE and Vicky Cropper of First Great Western, Bruce Thompson of Devon County Council and Richard Burningham MBE of Devon & Cornwall Rail Partnership. Thanks are also due to Barnstaple Town Council, Beverley Cole formerly of the National Railway Museum at York, Carol Coombs, Crediton Town Council, Tim Davies, Eggesford Garden & Country Centre, the Mare & Foal Yeoford, Michael Morant, the New Inn Coleford, Otter Brewery, Jasmine Rodgers of the Science & Society Picture Library, Steve Pospisil of Southern Posters, the Station Master's Café, Barnstaple, St. Austell Brewery, Tarka Rail Association Committee members John Burch, John Phillips and their colleagues, Kevin Freeborn, my editor at Crimson Publishing, and lastly surgeons Francis Wells and Vikram Devaraj, without whose skilled intervention I would not still be wandering the Devon footpaths in my eighth decade. The sketches of the stations, as once they were, are the work of Brian Siggery, while every page testifies to the expertise and enthusiasm of Touchwood Design's Emily Cobbledick.

FOREWORD

We walk in invisible footprints.

The footprints of tens of thousands of men and women who trod these winding paths and loved this soft wet landscape hundreds of years before we uttered our first cries. One of the pleasures of these walks is that, keeping an eye out for what they left behind, we come to know the owners of those footprints a little better.

Rural communities have long had a reputation for resisting change, of taking pride in their adherence to the old, time-honoured ways. The city dweller's dismissive description of his Devonshire country cousins as "a bunch of stick in the muds" contained more than a grain of truth. Indeed, mud lay at the very heart of the matter.

For centuries Devon's steep hills

Morchard Bishop's London Inn on the old Barnstaple to Exeter stage-coach route

and heavy rainfall gave its so called "roads" an infamous reputation. Trisdam Risdon, writing in 1630, described the lanes in the county's "hilly lands" as:

"very laborious and fatiguing, rough and unpleasant to Strangers unaccustomed to travel in such Ways; being cumbersome and uneven, in some Parts deep and miry, in others rocky and stony, painful for Man and Horse."

While William Chapple noted (1785):

"it was not without reason that the Devonshire Roads were formerly complained of... the Hills in many Places steep, the lanes everywhere narrow... so that Strangers, in the rainy Seasons, would rather take them to be watery Ditches than public Roads."

In Chapple's time travel by horseback still remained the best available option but, as we'll discover, this method of transportation was neither pleasant [Crediton: Walk 6] nor without risk [Morchard Road: Walk 4].

If travelling from one place to another was a challenge for the privileged few who had access to a horse, it was an infinitely more gruelling experience for the populace at large, who had no alternative but to leg it along footpaths or down muddy lanes. (The height of Devon's famous hedgerows, particularly on hills, is attributable to the fact that, in the days before tarmacadam, rainstorms repeatedly turned lanes into torrents of water and mud, destroying any semblance of road surface and further deepening the man-made passageways down the hillside.)

Along these primitive byways the very poorest went barefoot but, for those who could scrape together sufficient pennies, boots were a necessary and highly-prized possession. Little wonder then that as late as the early 20th Century every Devon village worthy of the name had, in addition to the blacksmith, at least one cobbler earning a life-long living from bootmaking and repair.

The great majority of country people rarely travelled farther afield than they could walk in a day. Generation after generation they lived, chose a spouse, raised children, worked and died within walking distance of their birthplace.

In rural Devon the winds of change moved slowly if at all, but it was clear by the end of the 18th Century that further east a transportation revolution was gathering momentum. Between 1760 and 1840 no fewer than 3,500 miles of canals -- a far more reliable means of transporting freight than any existing road -- were constructed.

The success of the canals prompted a fresh interest in road transportation and the formation of numerous Turnpike Trusts. These were private entrepreneurial ventures established to build roads designed for speed. Toll-houses were placed at intervals along the route to extract payment from users and so to reimburse the investors. [See King's Nympton: Walk 4].

Chulmleighs's 1849 Market House

Again and again in these pages we witness the impact, first of the Exeter to Barnstaple turnpike (1828-1831) and later of the North Devon railway line (1854) upon the surrounding communities. For these two great transportation projects came at a price, and that price was paid by dozens of villages and hamlets high above the valley.

Before the completion of the new turnpike, the main road from Exeter to Barnstaple, after leaving Crediton, had followed the ridgeway through Newbuildings, Morchard Bishop, Chawleigh and Chulmleigh. (The several "London Inns" along this highway, e.g. at Morchard Bishop [Morchard Road: Walk 1] and, until it was renamed in 1869, at Chawleigh [Eggesford: Walk 1] testify to the existence of this old stage-coach route from North Devon via Exeter to the capital.)

With the opening of the valley turnpike, the stage-coaches diverted to the new, level and much faster riverside road. Horse-drawn freight traffic followed. As a direct consequence Morchard Bishop's population plummeted in the 19th Century from 1,698 to 985. Seven miles to the North-west the larger hilltop town of Chulmleigh fought desperately to stem this migration of trade and transport down to the valley. [See King's Nympton: Walk 3]. In 1849 a "Market House", expressly intended to restore Chulmleigh's declining economic fortunes, was built in the centre of town, but by then the die was cast and the new building never saw the activity for which it was constructed. It stands today, disguised as the "1894" Town Hall, and few residents of Chulmleigh are aware of its original purpose.

If ridgeway communities found themselves fighting for their economic lives, valley settlements along the route of the turnpike and railway took a fresh lease on life. Copplestone offers an good example of the way in which a tiny hamlet prospered from the transportation revolution. Stroll around Copplestone today, and note that this is a village built mostly of bricks, the great majority of its houses constructed after 1860 when the turnpike and the railway were comfortably established. Copplestone: Walk 4, a favourite of the author, is of particular interest in that it provides an opportunity to compare the delightfully unspoiled village of Coleford, which never merited a railway station (though the railway skirts the village) and Copplestone, which was assigned a station and was transformed almost beyond recognition.

Nor was this an isolated case. Communities all over the country were faced with the decision of whether or not to welcome the railway and the hoards of, often drunken, navvies who arrived to build it. (Sussex residents can compare the architecture and economic fortunes of Hurstpierpoint, the little downland town that declined to be on the route of the London - Brighton railway line, and Hassocks which owes its existence to Hurstpierpoint's refusal.)

Today, it's hard to appreciate the profound effect these transportation changes had upon mid-Devon. Since the arrival of the turnpike and the railway, there were others hardly less momentous. The coming of tarmacadam and the invention of the pedal bicycle expanded the horizons of the agricultural labourer. In the 1920s omnibus companies put Exeter and the market towns of Barnstaple and South Molton within easier reach. Telephone and the wireless brought news from afar. The massive post-war increase in motor car ownership put an end to the isolation of even the most remote Devon hamlet (and then proceeded to threaten the county's elaborate railway network.)

Change continues. Riding the Tarka Line today, it's not uncommon to see luggage adorned with labels from airports half-way around the world. In Devon pubs, once hushed to overhear details of a day-trip with the carrier to Exeter, we can now pick up accounts of holidays spent in Thailand or San Francisco. Mid-Devon, floods and blizzards aside, is isolated no longer. A better world? Most would probably say "Yes."

But for those who are tempted to turn back the clock, to catch the scent of times long past, to walk for a few hours in those invisible footprints, the paths and byways of Devon's ancient heartland lie waiting.

Peter Craske
South Tawton, Devon
New Year's Day, 2013

Representing users of the Barnstaple to Exeter rail line

The Tarka Rail Association exists as an independent advocate on behalf of the line's users, and we fulfil this role by developing positive working relationships with the other stakeholders in the line. These include railway companies (principally Network Rail and the current train operator), local councils, multi-agency groups, such as the Tarka Line Forum and the Devon & Cornwall Rail Partnership and, most importantly for us, existing and potential users of the line and the communities it serves.

Recent efforts have resulted in additional services to fill gaps in the timetable, a late-night service on Fridays and improved bus/rail integration. In addition we have produced timetable leaflets and walks booklets for the benefit of users of the line.

For information on becoming a member please visit www.tarkarail.org

Join us today, and have your say!

The more members we have, the greater our influence!

journeydevon
your guide to public transport

Where are you going?

Need easy information to help you find your way?

Wherever you want to be, there are lots of ways to make getting around Devon easy:

- Ideas for great days out on the bus or scenic railways of Devon

- Great money-saving tips for the bus or train

- A fully interactive bus map showing routes and services across the county

- On-line e-books with the latest bus and rail timetables

For further information visit
www.journeydevon.info

Devon
County Council

60 TARKA LINE WALKS

Note: All walks are circular unless marked (OW) indicating one-way to the next station.

A great pint of beer is always near

Enjoy a pint of Otter wherever you are on the Tarka Line

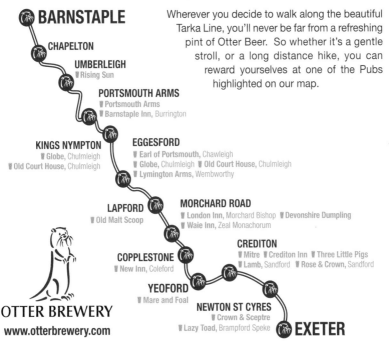

BARNSTAPLE

CHAPELTON

UMBERLEIGH
🍺 Rising Sun

PORTSMOUTH ARMS
🍺 Portsmouth Arms
🍺 Barnstaple Inn, Burrington

KINGS NYMPTON
🍺 Globe, Chulmleigh
🍺 Old Court House, Chulmleigh

EGGESFORD
🍺 Earl of Portsmouth, Chawleigh
🍺 Globe, Chulmleigh 🍺 Old Court House, Chulmleigh
🍺 Lymington Arms, Wembworthy

LAPFORD
🍺 Old Malt Scoop

MORCHARD ROAD
🍺 London Inn, Morchard Bishop 🍺 Devonshire Dumpling
🍺 Waie Inn, Zeal Monachorum

COPPLESTONE
🍺 New Inn, Coleford

CREDITON
🍺 Mitre 🍺 Crediton Inn 🍺 Three Little Pigs
🍺 Lamb, Sandford 🍺 Rose & Crown, Sandford

YEOFORD
🍺 Mare and Foal

NEWTON ST CYRES
🍺 Crown & Sceptre
🍺 Lazy Toad, Brampford Speke

EXETER

OTTER BREWERY
www.otterbrewery.com

Wherever you decide to walk along the beautiful Tarka Line, you'll never be far from a refreshing pint of Otter Beer. So whether it's a gentle stroll, or a long distance hike, you can reward yourselves at one of the Pubs highlighted on our map.

Come and see Crediton!

Explore our distinctive market town in the heart of Devon with its independent High Street shops and twice monthly farmers' market. Relax in our excellent cafés, restaurants and pubs. With 1400 years of recorded history, Crediton makes a great destination.

Crediton Town Council,
Market Street
01363 773717
www.crediton.gov.uk

Before or after your walk

The Mare & Foal, Yeoford

Just yards from the station
Open all day on Saturday
Home cooked food
(closed Monday lunchtimes)
Cask Marque accredited,
Children's Play Area, Dogs Welcome

Your hosts: Trevor & Jayne
01363 84348 www.mareandfoal.co.uk

12

Explore Devon & Cornwall
...by train

Devon & Cornwall have some of Britain's most scenic train trips.

Beat traffic queues and parking problems - park and ride at Liskeard for Looe and Lelant Saltings for St Ives.

The Looe Valley Line

The St Ives Bay Line

Barnstaple

DEVON

CORNWALL

Exeter
Exmouth

Liskeard
Gunnislake

Newquay
Par
Looe
Plymouth
Paignton

Truro

St.Ives

Penzance
Falmouth

Find out more with our QR code, visit www.greatscenicrailways.com or call in at a Tourist Information Centre or staffed station.

Devon & Cornwall
RAIL PARTNERSHIP

EXETER ST. DAVID'S

Located on a hill overlooking the River Exe (originally the *Isc* or *Isca*), Exeter is one of England's most historic cities, and much has been written about it. The river marked the western extremity of Roman influence, and though isolated outposts can be found further west [See Lapford: Walk 3.] the conquerors were mostly content to leave England's south-western peninsula to the *Dumnonii*, its original Celtic occupants. The bishopric was transferred from Crediton in 1050, a castle built in 1068, and over the next 800 years the port of Exeter grew to be among the most important in the country. Brunel's broad-gauge railway arrived in 1844.

Walk 1. Fluid Mechanics: Exwick to Double Locks. 6 miles. 3.5 hours.
The least rural walk in the series, but one whose river, flood channels, suspension bridges, weirs, quays, canals and locks will appeal to industrial archaeology enthusiasts (and dogs who like a dip!) The going is level and the walk can be shortened at any time simply by turning back.
Facilities: Refreshment rooms & shops at Exeter St. David's; riverside pubs along the route; shops and cafés at the Quay.

On leaving the station, turn left for 100 yards and, at the first corner, keep left through a car park to reach the manned (a rarity these days) Red Cow level crossing. Ahead lies the Riverside Goods Yard, (much enlarged to handle WWII traffic, but now a shadow of its former self.) Keeping a close eye on children and dogs bear left over the railway, almost immediately crossing the Exe and, just beyond, a sunken flood channel (constructed between 1965 and 1977 following a particularly devastating flood in October 1960). Turn left to follow the channel's farther bank past the Exwick playing fields and under the main line. Hug the bank for a further 0.2 miles to reach a footbridge beyond which the flood channel joins the Exe. Remain on the west bank which offers good views of Blackaller Weir and its stylish suspension footbridge. Not far ahead the path passes beneath the, often gridlocked, Exe bridge roundabout. The river

was supposedly fordable at this point, but lives were frequently lost attempting the crossing, and between 1190 and 1238 an 18-arch stone bridge, one of the first in England, was constructed. Its impressive remains may be viewed from the north side of the roundabout. Continue along the bank [SP Quay] to another suspension bridge. Cross over and turn right to reach Exeter's Quay with its cafés & shops.

In Roman times the Exe was navigable as far as Exeter, but early shipping activity centred on Topsham, four miles downstream. In 1284 Isabella de Fortibus constructed Countess Wear effectively cutting off the city from the sea, and in 1311 the Courtenay family, with mills along the river and commercial interests at Topsham, took further steps to prevent craft travelling upstream. In the mid-16th Century, following Henry Courtenay's 1538 execution

14

for conspiracy, John Trew was engaged to dig a canal to Exeter. His £5,000 project, the first pound lock canal in the country -- 1.77 miles in length, 16 ft. wide and three ft. deep -- was completed in 1566.

A century later Exeter "keye" was extended to the river and the purpose-built Custom House, Exeter's first brick building, was constructed. In 1724, the canal was extended to four miles in length, 59 ft. in width and 10 ft. deep, allowing vessels of up to 150 tons to use Exeter quay. Trade became brisk. Devon wool produced the highly-prized Exeter serge, much of it exported to Holland. The canal basin lies just across the river and (if you choose to linger here) can easily be reached by the suspension bridge you've just crossed.

Continue to the far end of the Quay and follow a pleasant elevated path (past a fine 1780 sandstone mill) for 0.2 miles to Trews Weir. Beyond lies a *third* suspension bridge constructed in 1935. Take this across the river and head for the decidedly more utilitarian bridge over another flood channel. Before you reach it, glance down at the left edge of the path. The parallel line of what, at first sight, appear to be iron bolts indicates one of many thousands of sites around the country from which railings were removed in 1939 and melted down for military re-use.

Beyond the flood channel is the Exeter Canal, peacefully sleeping away its retirement. Turn left and follow the old towpath past allotments and playing fields. In the 80 years prior to 1840 more than 3,500 miles of canals were built across the British countryside. Less

than two centuries ago this tranquil stretch of water would have been bustling with tow-horses, and their grimy successors: steam-powered boats.

At the swing bridge, cross over and continue for 0.5 miles to the Double Locks pub. The railway lies to your right. Its mid-19th Century arrival and its ability to transport freight at high speed sounded the death-knell of hundreds of canals like this one, leaving the man-made waterways much as we see them today, their stillness broken only by the splash of a duck or the barking of a dog.

Retrace your steps, along either bank.

EXETER ST. DAVID'S

On leaving the station, head for the double roundabout by the Great Western Hotel. Turn left into Red Cow village. At the traffic lights cross over and continue in the same direction along Cowley Bridge Road's elevated pavement which ends at a ramp leading up to New North Road. Cross with care to reach the high balustraded pavement and continue northwards. After a further 0.8 miles, at the Cowley Bridge traffic roundabout, cross the Tiverton-bound A396 with care, and follow the A377 [SP Crediton]. Stand for a moment on Cowley railway bridge. To the North, the Paddington main line curves gently right, while the North Devon (Tarka) Line -- demoted in 1965/7 to a single track -- heads left across the Exe.

Continue along the A377 facing the oncoming traffic. Exercise care: neither of the two river bridges ahead has a pavement. The first of these, built by Brunel, crosses the Exe. The final, graceful three-arch bridge was completed in 1814 by James Green at a cost of £9,000. It spans the waters of the River Creedy from Crediton (*Creedy-town*) and a portion of the flow from the Exe and Culm catchment areas. Plaques beneath both parapets commemorate the laying of the first stone.

Enter the village of Cowley, and take the first road to your right [SP Upton Pyne] crossing the Creedy and the Tarka Line. Some 300 yards beyond the railway bridge, turn in by the lodge and along the main drive to reach Pynes. The Pyne family have been Lords of the Manor since the time of Henry I. Their fine Queen Anne house, probably built by Sir Henry Northcote who married the Pyne heiress early in the 18th Century, was sensitively enlarged in 1851, but the arrival of the railway seven years earlier with its smoke-belching engines must have tarnished the family's tranquil view across the Exe.

At the home farm, your route (downgraded to a footpath) passes behind a piggery. Note the walled kitchen garden below the farm to your right. Continue ahead through the park with its massive oaks, to reach a wood guarded by the headless shaft of a granite cross. Beyond the wood continue ahead along the upper edge of a large water meadow, keeping an eye out for a green bridge to your right. When level with this bridge, at a footpath junction, turn right to reach Stafford railway bridge. **Stop, look and listen; trains here travel at high speed.** Taking *extreme care*, especially of children and dogs, cross the main line and accompany it over the river. On the far bank turn left along a track. Avoiding the metal gate to your right, keep left along the elevated footpath that follows the river bank upstream to meet the A396 at a stile.

Cross this main road with care, dog-legging 10 yards right to take an unsigned path into Stoke Woods. The path parallels the road before turning left uphill. Navigation is a trifle challenging. At the *first* intersection bear right and follow the blue track uphill. At the *second*, continue ahead and uphill. At the *third*, bear right and follow the steps uphill. At the *fourth*, turn left (blue route) up more steps to reach the car park and Pennsylvania Road. The mound opposite, around which you're about to walk, was once the site of an Iron Age hill fort. Turn left and follow the road for 150 yards to a signed footpath on your right leading over a cattle grid and up to Stoke Hill Farm. The view north up the Exe valley is breathtaking. At the farm turn right past a barn conversion and shortly right again along a signed bridleway that skirts the far side of the fort. After rain the going can be very muddy.

The 159 metre (522 ft) hill summit to your right was used by the Romans as a signal station. After 0.5 miles, the bridleway merges with a lane and shortly after rejoins Pennsylvania Road. Turn left, downhill. After 200 yards, take the first turning right into Argyll Road, immediately bearing hard right past three brick pillars, and left into Belvidere Road, which later degenerates into a permitted footpath (guarded by bollards) through private land. Follow it downhill ignoring all side paths. At the bottom beyond a second set of bollards, bear right along a gravel drive to reach a T-junction with Lower Argyll Road. Turn left downhill to Cowley Bridge Road. Turn left again and retrace your steps to the station.

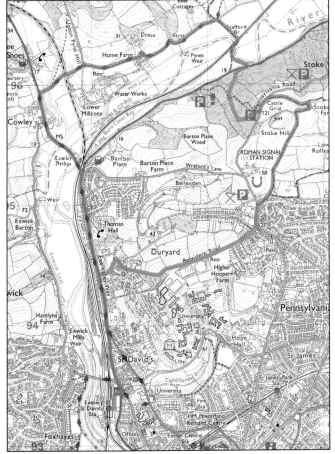

NEWTON ST. CYRES

Known before the Great War simply as "St. Cyres," the station suffered the disadvantage of being located a mile from the village it served. Yet its proximity to Exeter, in the gentler days before mass vehicle ownership, ensured a healthy number of ticket sales: 10,385 in 1928 -- a figure only surpassed by those of Barnstaple, Crediton and Yeoford. Today the situation is reversed. Few trains stop at the isolated station. Be warned that the drop from train to platform is very steep.

Walk 1. Hob-goblins and Holy Wells. 4.4 miles. 3 hours.
A pleasant walk along quiet lanes and footpaths through distinctive redland
farm country bordering the Raddon Hills.
Facilities: Pub at the station and at Shobrooke.

Note the bridge at the west end of the platform, its arch wide enough to take the two broad gauge tracks that served the station until 1892. At the crossroads directly outside the station, take unsigned Lake Lane north past two *cul-de-sac* signs. After 150 yards, watch for a footpath sign in the right-hand hedge. Take this path, which follows a fence, bypassing Lake Farm and ending at a road. Turn left into the road and follow it for 0.4 miles to Wyke Cross and a pair of estate cottages.

Turn right [SP Shobrooke Mill], passing more estate cottages and over Wyke Hill before dropping down to a sharp turn at Shobrooke Mill Farm. The present farm dates back scarcely more than 100 years, but in preceding centuries a bustling grain mill stood here, powered by the waters of Shobrooke Lake -- a grand name for so unassuming a stream. Leave the road at the farm and continue ahead along a signed track, initially following the course of the old mill leat. After 0.2 miles, do *not* climb

the stile but keep left, descending to cross the mill leat and stream by twin footbridges. Continue for a further 0.4 miles (with the stream now on your right) to reach a gated track leading to Shobrooke village.

Southern Railway claimed the resorts they served (even in Devon!) enjoyed better weather.

University of Nottingham etymologists suggest the name Shobrooke means Hob-goblins' Brook, and the village still retains an air of times past. Its most famous son was

Thomas Westcote, whose *View of Devonshire* provides historians with a rare glimpse of life in the county at the end of the 16th Century. But for the most part Shobrooke has been content to ignore the wider world, deriving its livelihood from the rich redland soil with which the parish is abundantly supplied.

Turn left and walk up the quiet main street. The pub is to your right. Some 200 yards beyond, take the footpath up steps in the left-hand bank and across a field to emerge at a lane. (Here, a few yards *up*hill in the right-hand hedge, stands a well-house. Restored in 1925, this is Shobrooke's Holy Well, one of more than 200 in the county. "Holy" is a relative term, for a spring existed here long before the coming of Christianity. The new church, placing as it did great store in baptism, would have been quick to oust lingering hob-goblins by conferring holy properties on an alternative water source lying so close to the church.)

London and South Western Ry.
787
TO
ST. CYRES

Turn left, *downhill*, to the church of St. Swithin. The Victorians undertook a massive rebuilding in 1880, but the Norman south doorway somehow escaped their attention. Note also the Lang memorial and the remains of an ancient preaching cross outside on the east wall. The cob wall along the churchyard's southern boundary is a more recent testament to Devon craftsmanship and local enthusiasm, sections having been expertly rebuilt as a community project in 2002.

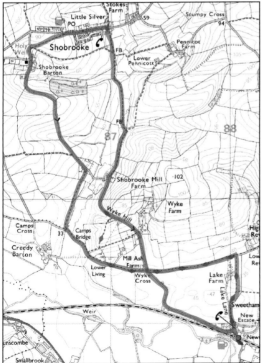

At the road junction by the church, continue briefly downhill with Shobrooke Barton's cob outbuildings on your left. (Note the barton's massive brick chimney to guard against thatch fires.) Follow this road for 0.6 miles. Beyond Mill Cottages, just before a bridge, turn right onto a signed footpath and proceed across three fields to reach a lane. Turn left over the stream and continue for 0.6 miles to Wyke Cross. A right-turn here brings you back to the station 0.5 miles distant.

NEWTON ST. CYRES

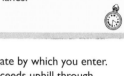

Walk 2. Circular walk to Upton Pyne. 5.3 miles. 3 hours.
A gentle walk along the Creedy valley to the village of Upton Pyne.
The outbound sections along the river bank can be muddy.
The return route is mostly by quiet country lanes.
Facilities: Pub at the station.

On leaving the station, turn left over the railway and, just before the ancient bridge over the River Creedy, turn left onto a footpath following the river bank downstream. After one mile, where a footbridge spans the river, cross the stile and immediately turn left away from the bridge and river bank along a footpath. This leads over the railway line (*be especially vigilant with children and dogs*) and across a field to a much smaller footbridge. Proceed over this and follow the path past two round hogan-like dwellings on the right to reach the site of the Langford Environmental Education Project and, immediately beyond, a road.

Turn right here and follow the road for 0.6 miles to New Bridge, where the road crosses first railway and then river. It was under the arches of this bridge towards the end of World War II, that three bedraggled German POWs were recaptured following their escape from a nearby internment camp.

Just before New Bridge, take a signposted footpath to the left past Oakford Lodge. About 100 yards beyond the lodge turn left off the drive by a large oak tree. A path leads uphill and then along field edges. Note the rapidly decaying cob wall in the hedge at the top of the second field -- evidence of what happens if cob, which can last for centuries, is left unprotected from the rain. At the end of the third field the path enters Lake's Down Wood, where there's a fine tree house just

to the left of the gate by which you enter. The path then proceeds uphill through gloomy conifers to reach a field. Follow the path across this field, past the rear of some modern houses, to the peaceful village of Upton Pyne.

The derivation of the village's name is fairly straightforward, "Up-town" indicating its elevated location on the northern side of Pynes Hill, a prominence overlooking the confluence of the Creedy and Exe rivers. Pyne is a reference to the local family who occupied the manor for ten generations following the reign of Henry I. Pynes, their ancestral home is a Queen Anne residence located at some distance from the village, close to the River Exe. [See Exeter: Walk 2.]

Built of local Raddon stone, the ancient church of Our Lady fully repays a visit. The distinguished Devon historian, W.G. Hoskins considered the outlook as one looks north from the churchyard over a gentle landscape inhabited since at least the bronze age to be "one of the most satisfying views in all Devon." The church is reached by a fine Devon cobblestone path. Note the ancient granite shaft just outside the south porch. The church tower, which dates from 1380, houses several statues in niches, those of David and Christ being the most easily recognisable. There are numerous memorials inside the church, many of them commemorating members of the Northcote family, who made their fortune from the local serge industry

and who have been associated with the area since the 16th Century. The horse trough in the street opposite the church forecourt offers further evidence of that family's close ties to the village.

In Victorian times, manganese ore was mined in the village at the Pound Living Mine -- known to locals as "the black pit." The row of cottages -- Belgrave Terrace -- just beyond the church on the left was built expressly to house the miners.

Continue along the lane that leads past the church, and after 0.3 miles at the Pye Corner junction take the left-hand fork and follow the lane for 0.6 miles, passing Little and Great Ley farms. Shortly after being joined by a lane from the right, and just beyond the bridge, take a footpath on the left which leads alongside a stream through a pleasant water meadow to a small bridge over a ditch. Cross the bridge and turn left into a larger field, following the edge clockwise around the field's perimeter to reach a road. Dog-leg slightly left across this road at Winscott Cross and take the lane almost opposite the footpath. This lane leads past Winscott Barton and Norton Farm to Newton St. Cyres station just 1.3 miles away.

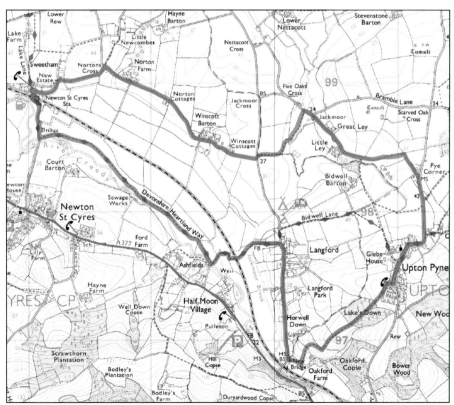

NEWTON ST. CYRES

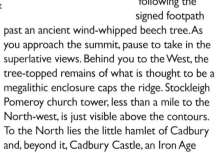

Walk 3. The Raddon Hills. 8 miles. 4.5 hours.
Save this lengthy outing for a fine day, not because the terrain is unduly difficult,
but the spectacular vistas are best enjoyed in good weather. The Raddon Hills offer
some of the finest views in Devon -- unequalled by any other walk in this series -- and
are guarded in spring by acres of apple blossom. Take your time ... and binoculars!
Facilities: Pub at the station.

On leaving the station, turn sharp right at the Station Cross fingerpost [SP Shute] and follow the lane for 0.25 miles to a T-junction [Nortons Cross]. Dog-leg slightly left to follow a signed footpath almost opposite. This leads along two field edges and a narrow pathway to emerge at a road corner. Proceed ahead past Newcombes and Churchills to an unsigned T-junction. Here dog-leg slightly right to rejoin the footpath, which bypasses a golf-course (newly constructed on prime farming soil) and continues in the same general direction uphill along a field edge and beside an orchard (the first of several you'll encounter). At the top of the orchard, bear right for 100 yards, to reach a gate where the path divides. Turn left through the gate following the field edge down to a lane. Turn right along this lane to reach an unsigned T-junction, and here turn left. Continue along this road for a mile, passing through Efford (possibly a corruption of East Ford) to a crossroads [Raddon Cross]. Continue ahead [SP Stockleigh Pomeroy] and steeply uphill for

Evidence of prevailing wind from the West

a further 0.7 miles to the hill crest and a scenic road junction.

You're now standing on the Raddon Hills, inhabited since at least the Bronze Age. Raddon stone, a variety of granite, has been in use locally for centuries. The churches at neighbouring Thorverton and Upton Pyne are both constructed of stone from these hills (though Newton St. Cyres's church procured its stone from Posbury, west of Crediton). Turn right along the unsigned lane for 200 yards. When the lane descends from the ridge, remain on the hill crest following the signed footpath past an ancient wind-whipped beech tree. As you approach the summit, pause to take in the superlative views. Behind you to the West, the tree-topped remains of what is thought to be a megalithic enclosure caps the ridge. Stockleigh Pomeroy church tower, less than a mile to the North-west, is just visible above the contours. To the North lies the little hamlet of Cadbury and, beyond it, Cadbury Castle, an Iron Age defensive mound.

After 0.4 miles, just beyond the 235 metre (770 ft) summit, proceed ahead at a footpath intersection and continue along the ridgeway path for a further 0.6 miles, passing a lone pine tree and crossing a stile. The views, equally magnificent, are now east across the Exe Valley to the distant Blackdown Hills, and south-west to Dartmoor. Descend gently to a second stile where steps lead down to another footpath junction. Bear right down a curving track which passes Raddon Hill Farm. Remain on the track as it winds its way down to a road running along the base of the hills. Turn right along this road. After a mile pass West Raddon, an ancient farming settlement mentioned in the Domesday Book. At the top of the rise beyond, dog-leg right at the crossroads and continue ahead [SP Shobrooke]. In about 0.6 miles, just beyond the brow of the hill [Exeter Hill Cross] turn left.

After 0.3 miles at (unsigned) Stumpy Cross, take the first turning to your right along a lane. Just beyond thatched Pennicott Farm, where the lane bends sharply

right, keep left on a signed footpath following a farm track along several field edges. At the bottom of the valley, cross two stiles in quick succession. Immediately beyond the *second* stile, turn left beside a dry leat to reach Shobrooke Mill Farm and a lane. Keep left along the lane and follow it for 0.4 miles over Wyke Hill and down to Wyke Cross. Continue ahead [SP Newton St. Cyres] for 0.5 miles to reach the station.

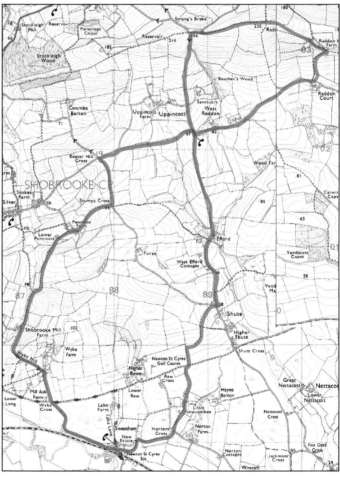

NEWTON ST. CYRES

Walk 4. The Five Woods. 7.5 miles. 5 hours.
A demanding walk along lanes, bridleways and footpaths ascending or descending
the five woods lying to the south of the village: Newton, Coombland, Whitestone,
Whiptail and Crooklake.
Facilities: Pub at the station. Pub (no dogs) & shop in the village.

Leave the platform and turn left over the railway bridge, shortly crossing the River Creedy. At the A377 junction turn left into Newton St. Cyres. Until the mid-20th Century, this was among the prettiest of Devon villages, with two rows of 16th and 17th Century thatched cottages tightly bordering the main road. The post-war increase in traffic led to severe congestion along the narrow main street and, after a prolonged public battle, the entire row of cottages along the south side of the street was demolished -- in the opinion of many, an act of public vandalism. Hints of the village's ancient charm are still to be found at the little ford and along the quiet lane that lies beyond.

Shuttern Brook, Newton St. Cyres

Cross first the main road and then the stream, Shuttern Brook, at the ford and proceed along Pump Street, which climbs past Lilly Farm to reach New Barn Cross. Turn right here. The lane ascends to Tinpit Hill -- a name testifying to earlier mining efforts -- and after 1.2 miles veers sharp left. At this point take the public bridleway that continues ahead up the hill. Coombland Wood lies to the right. The field on the left gives way at a muddy intersection to Newton Wood. Continue ahead and uphill. This rather austere portion of the route can be harder going after rain. Just before the summit, the canopy lightens sufficiently to permit a bluebell crop in the spring. At a gate, with a view of a radio tower ahead, the path emerges from the wood and follows a hedge, first on the left (with views to the encroaching outskirts of Exeter) and later on the right, where it soon borders the upper edge of a steep coomb. Perversely, this second field always manages to be wetter along its upper, bridleway edge than lower down. Obey the signs and stick to the upper hedge as best you can. At the far end of this field the bridleway reaches the Rowhorne Road.

Turn hard right onto the road to pass between Rowhorne and West Rowhorne farms. Just beyond the radio transmitter tower, at Waddlesdown Cross, proceed straight ahead and 0.3 miles further on

24

take a right-hand turn [SP Oldridge & Crediton]. After 0.3 miles this lane is joined at Twiscombe Corner by one from the left. Continue on, passing a track leading to Little Bowlish farm on the left. After a left-hand curve in the road, opposite Greenfields, take the signed footpath over the stile on the right.

In the spring this section along a grassy track is delightful with good views, primroses and violets in abundance. Where the footpath enters Whitestone Wood at a metal gate, follow the signed path left and downhill through Whiptail Wood. Less forbidding than the ascent to Rowhorne, this path offers wood anemonies in the spring, bilberries in season, and a couple of remarkable wood ant-hills, one of them over three feet in height.

The path descends steadily, at the bottom bearing right through a gate to join Shuttern Brook on its journey to the village. Keep the stream on your left and follow the path gently downhill, before turning upwards for the final few yards to emerge from the woods at a road. Turn left and follow this road downhill and over the brook. Continue for 0.8 miles, past Crooklake Wood on the left, to the crossroads just beyond Woodley Farm.

Turn right and descend Riscombe Hill to enter Newton St. Cyres's West Town. Shuttern Brook puts in its third appearance just to the right of the road. The church of St. Cyriac, built of local Posbury stone, dates mostly from the early 15th Century. It contains several memorials to the Northcote family, who made their fortune from wool and serge, and to the Quicke family of Newton House, best known today for their local cheese. The station, clearly signposted, lies 0.9 miles directly ahead and across the A377.

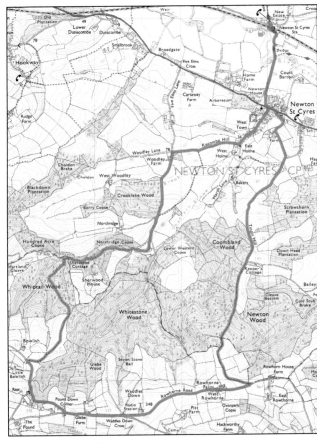

NEWTON ST. CYRES

Walk 5. Stockleigh Pomeroy. 8.2 miles. 5 hours.
A lengthy walk to an ancient Saxon settlement. Lovely views. In June, the hedgerows
are filled with the scent of honeysuckle and dog rose.
Facilities: Pub at the station and, just off the route, at Shobrooke.

From Station Cross take an unsigned road parallel to the railway passing the pub on your left. After 0.5 miles at Wyke Cross continue ahead over Wyke Hill to reach Shobrooke Mill, where the lane bends left. Follow a signed footpath *to the right* alongside the old mill leat. After 0.2 miles climb a stile on your right entering a field, only to leave it moments later via a second stile to the left. The path then follows field edges to emerge at a lane by Pennicott Farm.

Turn left and follow the lane for 0.2 miles to a T-junction. Take the signed footpath which continues ahead along the east side of the Shobrooke Lake (there is no lake!) valley past a massive oak. As

Raddon Hills' residents above Parsonage Copse

the route bears right along the base of a gently rounded hill, be alert for a footpath sign at a gate *below you on the left.* Your route now heads north, crosses a lane and ascends to enter Stockleigh Wood. Emerging from the trees at a footbridge, follow the field edge uphill to a gate on the ridge. Here, on the western extremity of the Raddon Hills, the views are spectacular. Go through the gate but *avoid the ridge, keeping left along the hedge* to a gate guarding Parsonage

Copse. Walk downhill through the wood, at the bottom bearing left to Stockleigh Pomeroy's ancient church.

Stockleigh derives from *Stocc Leah* -- a woodland clearing protected by a log stockade. The size of the original Saxon enclosure may be determined by a short diversion around the village's ancient "Green". After the Norman Conquest (1066) the manor, formerly owned by a Saxon, Alveva, was given to the Norman Ralf de Pomaria (hence *Pomeroy*) in reward for his efforts at the decisive battle of Hastings (1066). The Domesday Book (1086) tells us that, by then, enough land had been cleared to permit the operation of six ploughs. On the home farm Ralf's bailiff supervised 103 sheep, 23 goats, 14 pigs, five cows and a *rouncey* -- a horse for his own transportation. By 1293 a water mill had been built, but for three long centuries beginning in 1348 Stockleigh Pomeroy, like many another Devon village, had its aspirations thrown into disarray by the repeated ravages of the Black Death. [W.G. Hoskins's *Devon and its People* includes a fascinating

chapter about the village and the milestones marking its economic development.]

Bearing this ancient history in mind, stroll clockwise round the Green, turning right just beyond the church and keeping right at all road junctions until you find yourself back at St. Mary's. The church dates from about 1150, and may have replaced an earlier wooden structure. After reaching the church for the second time, continue on to the next bend but now *turn left*, downhill to the A3072. Dog-leg a few paces right and *cross with care* following a signed footpath on the far side down to a stream. Cross, immediately bearing briefly right, upstream, on the far bank to reach an ancient tree-lined way leading gently uphill. Signage is poor and the first "short-cut" footpath option is hard to spot, so stay right along the field edge to a well-marked path junction. Here turn left along the edge of three fields to reach a brick cottage and a lane -- the outskirts of Chilton. [Don't try to lengthen the walk by returning through Trew Woods further west. The footpath is poorly signed and abysmally maintained!]

Turn left beyond the cottage following the lane downhill to the pleasant bustle of Westwood Farm. *Carefully* re-cross the A3072, just beyond, to join a signed footpath accompanying Shobrooke Lake to a quiet lane. Dog-leg 35 yards left across this lane and, at the footpath junction on the far side, take the *left-hand* fork across two water meadows. At a footpath T-junction in the third field, turn left towards Moor Farm and continue along its entrance drive to Shobrooke. (The pub lies halfway up the village street on the right).

If you're not visiting the Red Lion, cross the street and continue along the footpath with the stream still to your left. Roughly 0.4 miles later, beyond twin footbridges, you'll spot the first

stile you encountered. *Don't cross it*, but continue alongside the mill leat to Shobrooke Mill and a road. Bear left, uphill, and retrace your steps to the station.

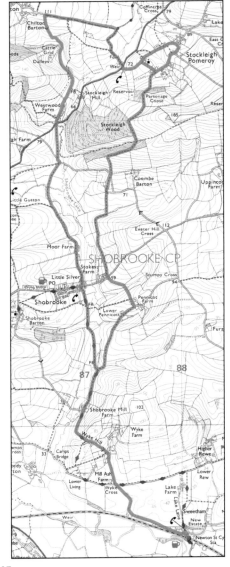

CREDITON

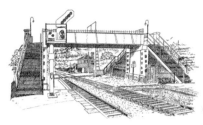

Though the line between Exeter and Crediton was completed early in 1847, legal wrangling delayed the railway's opening for four years. Crediton has been a recognised centre since Saxon times. In the early 8th Century the town's most famous son, Winfrith (later St. Boniface), converted much of Europe to Christianity. Crediton's first church built in the early 10th Century served for 150 years as a cathedral, before the bishop's throne was moved to Exeter. From the 13th to the 17th Centuries the town was a noted wool centre. With the decline of the serge industry, Crediton diversified into other agricultural products and became famous for its cider, produced in mills located just beyond the Exeter end of the "up" platform. The town was twice devastated by fire in the 18th Century.

Walk 1. Putting Greens & Peacocks. 3.3 miles. 2 hours.
One of the shortest walks in the series and among the least demanding.
The Crediton Station Tearooms provide an ideal end-of-walk reward for children.
Facilities: Pubs and shops in Crediton; Tearooms (closed Sundays) at Crediton station.

Leave the station by the "down" (Barnstaple departures) platform, and immediately turn left opposite the car park to follow the railway line away from the level crossing and past a small industrial estate in the direction of Exeter. The road ends at a footpath which veers right and enters the manicured grounds of Downes Crediton Golf Course. Take care of children and dogs. A well-marked footpath leads across the golf course and over the River Yeo at the brick-sided Kersford Bridge. Dippers may sometimes be glimpsed along the banks of the river.

On the far side of the bridge turn half-left and make for a large wooden pole supporting a power line in the middle of the fairway across from the Club House. From this pole the path leads around the left-hand edge of a small lake and then skirts the edge of Hookway Down Wood, just to the left, before reaching a lane. Turn left into this lane, still keeping the wood on your left. Ignore the lane that branches off to the right, but continue ahead and uphill between high earthen banks. Just beyond the steepest portion of the ascent, keep an eye out for a footpath sign in the right-hand hedgerow giving onto a track.

Turn right onto this track and follow it gradually uphill. There are pleasant views to the East. Some 300 yards beyond the crest of the hill, be aware of a small community below the track to your right. At a misleading sign on the left of the track, *turn right* down a green lane. This can be muddy after rain. Descend steeply to reach Hookway Farm, nestling in a little valley. Just beyond the farm

HIKE for HEALTH
SOUTHERN RAILWAY
Go-as-you-please cheap tickets
get you to the country quickest

Ask for details at any S.R. Office and buy
"Southern Rambles" by S.P.B.Mais 6d

DEVON (SR)

there is a crossroads of sorts. At this junction, turn left past Glover Cottage, and through a gate.

Weir at Fordton

Keep the hedge on your right as you proceed uphill to reach Rudge Farm, a pleasant brick-built Georgian farmhouse. In addition to noisy dogs and chickens, the farm has an active dovecote and some highly decorative peacocks. Note the wheel extending through the barn wall. In years gone by this would have been connected by a canvas belt to a steam traction engine parked outside and providing power for such major chores as threshing or log sawing. Beyond Rudge, the footpath veers right and continues along a pleasant track offering fine views to reach a lane. Turn right into the lane and follow it mostly downhill for 0.6 miles to reach a crossroads [Fordton Cross].

Continue ahead at the crossroads, passing Fordton House and its carefully maintained gardens to your left before recrossing the River Yeo at Fordton Bridge. Note the cutwaters set into the bridge's upstream side. These enable the piers of the bridge to slice easily into the current, in much the same way as the bow of a ship, and also provide a refuge for pedestrians. Just upstream from the bridge there is a pleasant weir and the river bed has been beautifully surfaced with stone.

Downstream are the old Fordton Mills, which once produced rough cotton sailcloth and coarse linens -- something of a departure for Crediton, whose chief commercial claim to fame until the late 18th Century was as a *woollen* town and a centre for the manufacture of woollen serge. Note that immediately beyond the old bridge are two modern "land arches" -- additional openings built over the water meadow to relieve pressure on the ancient bridge in time of flood. Modest cutwaters have also been provided on the modern section, both on the up- and (purely for decorative purposes) down-stream sides.

From the bridge, Crediton station lies 0.2 miles straight ahead. All the Station Tearoom's baked items, teacakes excepted, are home-made. Traditional Devon junket with nutmeg and clotted cream is usually available. There are also some interesting old photographs and a small model railway exhibit.

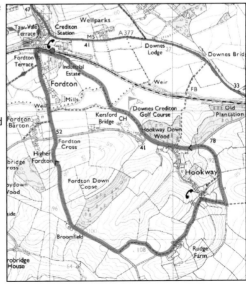

CREDITON

Walk 2. Salmonhutch and Posbury. 6.4 miles. 3.5 hours.
A gentle beginning alongside the River Yeo gives way to some exertion as the route
ascends to Posbury. Lovely views. Some sections can be muddy after rain.
Facilities: Pubs and shops in Crediton;
Tearooms (closed Sundays) at Crediton station.

Walk to the level crossing. Turn left away from the town immediately entering Fordton, and look for a signposted track opposite a row of cottages. Turn right here and follow a pleasant footpath between the railway line and the River Yeo. At the first kissing gate, stay left. After 0.8 miles the path reaches a quiet lane. Immediately to your right lies the Salmon Pool level crossing. When the BBC was gathering oral histories for an archive of wartime memories, a delightful contribution was made

Posbury Clump from the lane above Upper Uton Cross

© John Craske

by Brian Cox, then a child of 12, the son of the crossing keeper. He recalled this remote crossing being blocked for almost two hours by a seemingly endless convoy of American armoured vehicles, much to the frustration of the Southern Railway.

Turn left, away from the level crossing, to cross the river and pass Salmonhutch Coarse Fishery. Avoid the left turn just beyond Uton Barton. Instead, bear right round the corner to enter Uton (pronounced *Yewton*, and

clearly a corruption of Yeo-Town). At Uton Village Cross turn left and proceed uphill for 0.8 miles to Posbury Clump, a stand of trees along the south-west horizon. Beyond, on the left, lies the isolated mid-Victorian chapel of St. Luke. An ancient quarry, now disused, provided stone for buildings as far distant as Newton St. Cyres. This remote location has in its time known both peace and war. Posbury is still home to a nunnery founded in 1934 and dedicated to St. Francis. Historians are generally agreed that the earthworks a few hundred yards to the South-west are the most likely location of the Battle of Posentesburh (661 A.D.) at which Cenwalh, Saxon King of Wessex, defeated the Britons, driving them off the fertile redlands.

At the chapel turn right along a narrow track, which later becomes a footpath and leads downhill along field edges to join a lane at Gunstone Mill. Turn right into the

lane and follow it across the Yeo and the railway beyond to reach a T-junction. Turn right here and 0.3 miles further on, at the fork, keep right to Follymoor where the lane bends sharply right. At this corner, leave the lane continuing straight ahead over a stile marked by a footpath sign.

Two footpaths begin here. Avoid the narrow canyon to your left but proceed ahead up the bank to a gate opening onto a field. Follow the field edge ahead along the lower slopes of the hill to reach Denbury Farm whose outbuildings have clearly seen better days. Follow the footpath past the farm and along two more field edges to Beare Mill Farm. At this point the footpath descends to a drive connecting the farm with the public road. Bear left and follow this drive to a T-junction.

Cross the lane here and take the steps up the bank directly opposite. These lead to a stile and a steep hillside. Aim for the first power pole ahead and slightly to your left, and continue upwards making for the highest field corner. The climb up "Heartbreak Hill" is steep but short with good views. At the top corner, go through the gate and follow the upper hedge of the field beyond, at the end of which there is a gate on your right. Pass through, noting the fine thatched longhouse two fields distant (and the distinctly less fine school buildings to the right). Follow the footpath to reach the longhouse and, beyond, the town of Crediton with its shops and pubs. The station lies 0.5 miles distant at the lower end of the town, off the main A377 road to Exeter directly behind the Shell petrol station.

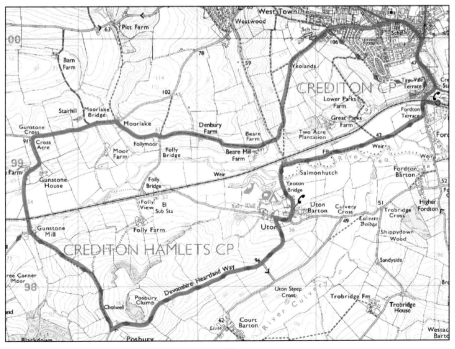

CREDITON

Walk 3. Yeo & Culvery Valleys. 6.6 miles. 4 hours.

The route ascends, through a succession of soil colours,
to a high ridge offering superb views.

Facilities: Pubs and shops in Crediton; Tearooms
(closed Sundays) at Crediton station.

Walk to the west end of the station by the level crossing. The signalbox, the last remaining on the line, dates from 1875 and marks the recommencement of single-line working; all Barnstaple-bound trains now being required to move over to the more northerly track. Alighting passengers can witness a time-tested safety procedure to prevent two trains meeting head-on: to access the line ahead, drivers exchange a token with the signalman, thus providing tangible evidence that the single track just vacated is now available for trains travelling in the opposite direction.

Turn left away from the town immediately entering Fordton, and after 200 yards look for a signposted track leading to the right opposite the row of cottages. Turn right to reach a pleasant footpath that makes its way between the railway line and the north bank of the River Yeo. At the first kissing gate, keep left and follow the hedge beyond. After 0.8 miles the path emerges onto a quiet lane. Turn left over the river to pass Salmonhutch Coarse Fishery which specialises in carp. Just beyond Uton Barton, avoid the left turn but bear right past a decaying cob wall to enter the tiny hamlet. (There is a Holy Well here, Ladywell, but it lies on private property.) At Uton Village Cross

turn left [SP Posbury] and, after 0.3 miles at Upper Uton Cross, left again down to Uton Steep Cross. Turn right here, noting the earth colour (You're about to leave the highly-prized red Permian sandstone soil and enter the Culm measures -- a hard sandstone interspersed with softer shale and clay) and continue to the little hamlet of Venny Tedburn.

Here, just beyond Court Barton, a large property on the left, lies a footpath separating the barton from neighbouring Cidercourt. Note the shaft of an ancient cross set into the wall of the latter property. The horizontal stone at the base of the shaft, which centuries ago may well have served as a wayside altar, has in the last century seen service as a repository, not for bread and wine, but for milk-churns awaiting collection by lorry. Continue ahead for another 0.2 miles. Just beyond Heddons, take the track ("Unsuitable for Motors") leading off to your left to ford the River Culvery. (A footbridge keeps your feet dry.) Wild brown trout are plentiful in the stream, whose name is possibly a local variation of *culverhay* -- "culver" being a pre-mediaeval word for the wood pigeon and "hay" meaning a house or homestead. If you fancy an alternative possibility, Culvery could equally well be a corruption of *culver-key* -- another name for the cowslip. Take your pick!

The track ascends steadily, with increasingly good views to the North (where the

southern edge of the Permian sandstone is readily apparent) to arrive, after 0.9 miles, at Oldridge Farm. Just beyond, on the right, stands an isolated chapel built in the mid-19th Century and designed by John Medley, a leader of the Oxford Movement. The Oldridge estate has ancient beginnings. Listed in the Domesday Book (1086 A.D.) as having belonged to a Saxon named Doda from whom the lands were appropriated, his name lived on. The next section of the walk along Oldridge Road is still locally referred to Doda's Ridge or Doddridge.

At the Oldridge Church fingerpost continue uphill [SP Exeter] to Tomhead Cross. Turn left here and, mindful of the Saxon footprints in which you are now walking, follow the ridge for 0.8 miles. The views to the North, and to the South-west across Tedburn St. Mary to the Teign Valley and Dartmoor, are spectacular. Just past a wind pump take the signed footpath to your left, bearing right at a large oak and passing a barn (with peacocks,

so keep dogs under control) to emerge at Copperwalls Lodge, which enjoys a glorious view east across the Exe valley. Turn left into the lane, and follow it (past abundant wild strawberries) for 1.8 miles, re-entering the red Permian sandstone soil shortly before Fordton Cross.

Here, continue straight on. The name Fordton -- *ford town* -- clearly pre-dates the ancient bridge. Note the fine cutwaters allowing the piers to slice cleanly into the current, while providing a refuge for pedestrians. The station (and its tearoom!) await you 0.2 miles ahead.

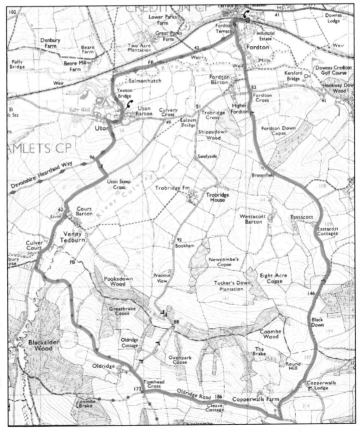

33

CREDITON

Walk 4. Yeo and Creedy valleys. 8 miles. 5.5 hours.
Despite Crediton's expansion, the nearby lanes and footpaths retain a timeless feel.
A demanding hike with a deceptively gentle beginning.
Facilities: Pubs and shops in Sandford & Crediton;
Tearooms (closed Sundays) at Crediton station.

Walk to the level crossing and turn left into Fordton. After 200 yards, take a signed lane on the right. This becomes a pleasant footpath well supplied with kissing gates (keep left at the first of these) along the north bank of the Yeo. After 0.8 miles the path reaches a lane. Turn right across the bridge (once spanning a mill leat outflow) and, *with care*, the level crossing.

After 250 yards, turn left to Beare Mill Farm. Behind the farm, at the top of the rise, head right up the bank and follow a footpath along field edges to reach Denbury Farm's ancient outbuildings. On the far side of the next field a gate leads down to a lane. Bear slightly right and follow this lane for 0.2 miles to an intersection [Moorlake Cross]. Proceed straight at this junction along a footpath which follows the valley to a delightful thatched cottage complete with apple orchard and vegetable garden. Turn left, uphill along a road. After 200 yards turn right into a signed lane leading (past, of all things, *electric* gates) to Hollacombe farm and its pleasant lake. Behind the farm the track follows the valley bottom finally crossing the stream (just a ditch in summer). On the far side, stay alert for a row of power lines. Turn right *up the last field edge before reaching them,* to the A377 -- Lord Portsmouth's 1828 Turnpike road between Exeter and Barnstaple.

Cross this busy road with *extreme care*, making for the footpath's continuation

50 yards to your left in the opposite hedge. Climb past Jewsmoor to another road, and continue straight across along a farm track. At 145 metres (475 ft), the brow of the hill offers a place to rest and take in a view extending to the Raddon Hills. Descend the track to Aller Barton and its cobbled yard. Birds now nest in the cob walls and there are lovely old outbuildings. Beyond, at a bend, turn right along a quiet lane which, in the days before his Lordship's turnpike, was the old main road between Exeter and Barnstaple. The colossal oak in the left hedge once looked down on foot and horse traffic which included the London stagecoach. After 0.4 miles, beyond a gentle double bend, take a footpath in the left-hand hedge, leading (through a succession of Heath Robinson gates utilizing everything from tyres to bailing twine) to Ruxford Barton, largely rebuilt in the 17th Century but dating back to Saxon times. At the end of the barton's entrance track, turn right onto a lane.

The attractive village of Sandford lies ahead. Note Town Barton on your right and the Victorian village pump to your left. The imposing classical school buildings date from 1825 and were erected by Sir Humphrey Davie of nearby Creedy Park. The church of St. Swithin repays a look both outside and in. There is fine cobblestoning along the raised pavement outside and more cobbles lie inside the church gate. In the best biblical

tradition, the visitor is instructed to enter the church "by the narrow door" which leads to an interior greatly enlarged in 1847. The carved pew ends date from the late 16th Century, and the fine west gallery from 1657. Seating in the gallery was intended for children from the local poorhouse, which may go some way to explaining its decidedly Spartan feel. There are numerous memorials to the Davie family.

As you descend the main street towards Crediton, 20 yards beyond Rose & Crownhill cross, look for a footpath on the left. Take this path through a graceful gate and past ancient sycamores for 0.3 miles to a lane.

Turn right and follow the lane between the River Creedy (unseen) on your left and Creedy Park (partly unseen behind its wall) on the right. For 400 years this was the home of the Davie family, standing in almost as many acres of manicured parkland. The 17th Century house was destroyed by fire in 1915 and rebuilt in the neo-Tudor style, only to be destroyed *again* in 1947. At the lodge gates bear left along an avenue of oaks and, at the next junction, keep right up the hill to Red Hill Cross. Turn left here shortly following an elevated footpath downhill to Crediton. The station is on the Exeter road just behind the Shell petrol station's forecourt.

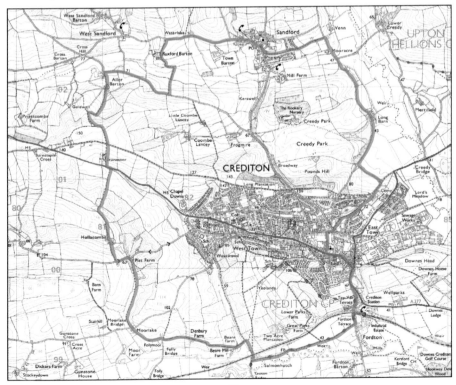

CREDITON

Walk 5. Upton Hellions & the Creedy Valley. 7.4 miles. 4.75 hours.
A gentle start gives way to hillier walking in remote countryside
above the River Creedy. Lovely views.
Facilities: Pubs and shops in Crediton;
Tea-rooms (closed Sundays) at Crediton station.

Walk to the level crossing and turn right to the intersection with the busy A377. *Cross it carefully,* turn left and follow the main road (past an ancient cob wall on the left) to the brow of the hill. Keep right at the road fork to enter Mill Street and walk against the one-way traffic flow. After passing Morrisons and Mole Avon on the left, bear right along the main road [SP Tiverton] before turning right into Commercial Road [SP Sports Centre]. Take the first left to the Centre's car park. Stay left and follow a signed footpath past tennis courts and across Lord's Meadow (the field where Charles I reviewed his troops in 1644 at the height of the Civil War). On the far side of the Meadow (after crossing a former mill leat and the River Creedy) the path emerges at a road corner. Turn left and follow this road along the edge of Shobrooke Park as far as the A3072. Carefully dog-leg 20 yards left across this main road and continue along a lane [SP Upton Hellions].

Nowadays on entering a town we take it for granted that we'll encounter newer buildings on the outskirts, and older structures as we approach the town centre. There's a similar, but much less well known, *rural* rule of thumb. As we head into remote Devon farm country, this is as good a place as any to record the fact that farms located near water in valley bottoms are usually of greater antiquity than those sited on the higher ground that was deforested later. (A bit of information, perhaps, worth filing away for use on our 59 other walks!)

Haske Barton

At the first fork [Lower Haske Cross] turn right and continue for 0.4 miles to a rural intersection. Here stay on the "main" road bearing left downhill and passing just right of a fine thatched longhouse [Haske Barton] with lovely cob outbuildings. About 80 yards beyond, by a circular drinking trough, keep right, up a signed bridleway. The OS map is out of date, and the route now involves a brief diversion, right to some barns, before the uphill climb continues. Follow the route markers, ascending steeply before a roller-coasterish section near the summit.

At the entrance to a wood the path bears right and joins a lane. Turn left and follow this lane through the Bremridge Estate

HIKE for HEALTH
SOUTHERN RAILWAY
Go-as-you-please cheap tickets
get you to the country quickest

Ask for details at any S-R Office and buy
'Southern Rambles' by S-P-B-Mais 6d

DEVON (SR)

before descending to the Creedy valley. Just before Heath Bridge over the river, turn left onto a signed footpath [SP Bremridge Farm] and, ignoring side paths, keep left up a long concrete drive to reach the farm. Stay to the right, and follow footpath signs for a further 0.4 miles over the hill brow before

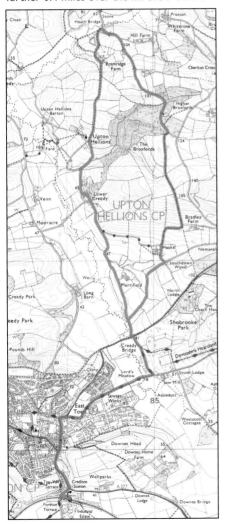

descending to the tiny village of Upton Hellions (*higher town*, of William de *Helihun*, 1242), a church and little more.

At the bottom of the footpath, bear hard right to reach St. Mary's lych gate and a delightful path of Devon cobbles. The church itself, still without electricity, is a model of stark simplicity. The chancel and nave date from the late 12th Century, and the arch above the south door is Norman. There's a lovely wagon roof with carved bosses. The south porch was built about 1400, while the tower, housing a single bell, is late 15th Century. In 1850 the population totalled a scant 146 -- much the same as today.

Interestingly, in 1642 (two years before Charles I reviewed his troops at Lord's Meadow) the men of Upton Hellions appear to have possessed a surprising degree of literacy, two in every five being able to sign his own name when asked to append it to the Protestation Oath. (Only one in three men at nearby Shobrooke could manage this feat!) Of women, who were not required to sign the oath, alas we know nothing.

Leave the church as you entered, but outside the lych gate turn left and immediately right, downhill, along a quiet road. At the second intersection [Lower Creedy Cross] continue ahead [SP Shobrooke] for a further 1.5 miles to rejoin your outbound route just before the staggered crossroads with the A3072. Dog-leg 20 yards left over this main road taking particular care of children and dogs, and retrace your steps past Shobrooke Park to Lord's Meadow. Turn right over the Creedy and across the Meadow, and return to the station.

CREDITON

Walk 6. Fire! Fire! One-way to Newton St. Cyres. 4.3 miles. 2.75 hours.
Newton St. Cyres's limited weekday train service makes
this a good Sunday outing (with the goal of a pub lunch very much in mind!)
Facilities: Pubs & shops in Crediton; Tea-rooms (closed Sundays)
at Crediton station. Pub at Newton St. Cyres station.

(Newton St. Cyres)

Head for the level crossing. Cross the road at the signal box and, just to its right, follow Four Mills Lane uphill to a cob wall above the Crediton-bound traffic. At the top of the rise, cross over, noting the fine Victorian post office (now closed), and continue past "No Entry" signs into Mill Street walking against the traffic flow. Keep along this road [SP Tiverton], which bears right near the edge of town. Turn right into Commercial Road [SP Sports Centre], taking the first turning left into the Sports Centre car park. Stay left to join a signed footpath leading past tennis courts to the Lord's Meadow recreation grounds. Two footbridges in succession take you first over an old mill leat and then the River Creedy to a road. Turn left and follow this road along the western boundary of Shobrooke Park.

Of Crediton's three great houses only Downes, the ancestral home of the Buller family, still survives. Creedy Park, the Davie family home north of the town was twice devastated by fire. [See Crediton: Walk 4.] Shobrooke Park, long associated with the Shelley family, did wartime duty as a boys' preparatory school relocated from the Home Counties to the safety of Devon. Early on the morning of 23rd January, 1945 a fire broke out, destroying the telephone line. One of the boys ran the mile into Crediton in his night-clothes to raise the alarm but, by the time the fire crews arrived, the building was an inferno, in which two boys lost their lives.

After 0.4 miles, at an iron gate, turn right into Shobrooke Park (laid out about 1845 by a Shelley cousin, Henry Hippisley-Tuckfield, whose family also had close associations with Posbury. See Yeoford: Walk 3.) Head half-right up to the lake. To reduce stress among the sheep, the sole remaining beneficiaries of

First Impressions Count! Shobrooke Park's south gatepost

Hippisley-Tuckfield's landscaping, keep dogs leashed in their presence. Walk briefly by the lake in an anti-clockwise direction. Beyond the cricket pitch, but before the bridge, head right beneath massive oaks towards the South Lodge and its huge ornamental gateposts. About 150 yards before reaching it, turn left up a 0.5 mile-long avenue of lime trees. At the upper end, take the side gate to the right

38

HIKE for HEALTH
SOUTHERN RAILWAY
Go-as-you-please cheap tickets
get you to the country quickest
Ask for details at any S-R Office and buy
'Southern Rambles' by S-P-B-Mais 6 D

DEVON (SR)

(immediately crossing a road) and follow the unsigned lane directly ahead.

This quiet lane evokes a pleasant sense of times past. It's tempting to wax lyrical about days gone by, but before the advent of tarmacadam remote Devon lanes like this one had an infamous reputation. As one 19th Century Devon squire observed, it was "certainly no joke riding out at night with a pair of lanterns fixed on underneath your stirrups to guide you in the dark ... Travelling by coach was not so very much better," especially if you were seated outside exposed to the full force of the elements. Today's pub place-mats, with their images of lusty men blowing on horns and ostlers leaping to hold the reins, provide us with a decidedly rose-tinted picture of coach travel. A further inconvenience was the fact that stage-coach guards, drivers and ostlers all expected a tip -- an expense that added about 25% to the published fares. (The railway companies wisely forbade mandatory gratuities.)

About 0.4 miles after leaving Shobrooke Park, turn left onto a footpath leading along field edges to another lane. Turn right and follow this lane down to Shobrooke Lake (a river!) before heading past Shobrooke Mill and up Wyke Hill. Towards the brow, take a signed footpath on the right which leads down, then up over two stiles to a grassy hill-top. Pause to take in the view. Looking to your right, you can make out Downes. Ahead of you, across the Creedy, stand two 19th Century transportation projects, which transformed forever what was once a quiet valley: the 1828 turnpike (a custom-built road that charged tolls to recoup its promoters' investment -- today's A377) and the railway (opened for passenger traffic to Crediton in 1851, to Barnstaple in 1854.)

From the hilltop head down, aiming just right of two cottages, where a gate leads through an orchard to a lane. Turn left along this lane to Wyke Cross, and here head right [SP Newton St. Cyres] to the station (and those pub place-mats!) only half a mile distant.

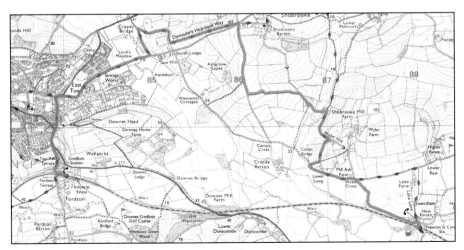

YEOFORD

Alighting at Yeoford today, it's hard to conceive that this station was once a significant railway junction, whose booking office even as late as 1928 was still issuing close to 13,000 tickets a year. Built a stone's throw from the confluence of the rivers Troney and Yeo, "Yeoford Junction" station featured, across from the existing platform, a central island platform with a refreshments room catering to the needs of passengers transferring between the North Devon line and the track which provided access to Okehampton, Tavistock, Plymouth, and the remote villages of west Devon and north Cornwall. Evidence of the steps leading up to the road bridge from these platforms can still be seen on the east side of the bridge parapet. Cattle pens, numerous sidings and a five-tonne crane once testified to the station's importance.

Walk I. Woodland Head and Yeo valley. 4.9 miles. 3 hours.
Almost entirely along quiet country lanes, this walk is suitable after rain. There are some steep hills.
Facilities: Pub in Yeoford. Library at Yeoford station.

On leaving the platform, turn right immediately crossing the River Troney. At the Yeoford Village intersection, just beyond the pub, bear right [SP Crediton & Exeter] and ascend the hill with its distinctive red sandstone banks. Visitors to Devon are often struck by the

Lanes deepen on steep hills

height of the county's hedgerows, particularly on hills. The explanation is simple: before the advent of tarmacadam (a mixture of slag and tar) in the early 20th Century, road surfaces were entirely unprotected from the elements. Year after year Devon downpours turned many a lane into a torrent of water, gouging out the soil and further deepening the man-made passageway down the hillside. Upgrading with the new surface was a slow and expensive undertaking, and one imagines that the little lanes around Yeoford ranked near the bottom of the Council's priority list.

Once the lane has levelled out, just beyond Hunterswood, be on the watch for a footpath sign leading down a farm lane to the right. Turn right here and follow the path diagonally across a field on the left, to join a second lane leading to the tiny hamlet of

Neopardy. At the road turn right, noting the wonderfully crooked first floor window in the neighbouring cottage, and descend once again to the river. Having united with the Troney a stone's throw from the Yeoford station platform, this river is now the Yeo, and will remain so until joining the Creedy a few miles further east at Crediton (*Creedy-town*). Cross the railway line and at the crossroads [Lower Neopardy Cross] turn right [SP Cheriton Bishop].

After 0.5 miles turn right again at Winstode Cross [SP Woodland Head & Yeoford] over a small stream before ascending steeply for 0.9

miles to reach Woodland Head Cross, at 156 metres (512 ft) the highest point on the walk. Note the delightful, almost unaltered, row of cottages ahead.

Bear right at Woodland Head Cross [SP Yeoford & Crediton] and, after 0.1 miles, continue straight ahead at Woodland Crossroads [SP Hittisleigh]. For the next 1.1 miles enjoy the views along this roller-coasterish lane which, after recrossing the River Yeo and a final climb, brings you to the T-junction at East Studham Cross. Turn right [SP Yeoford]. The railway station lies a mile away and gently downhill.

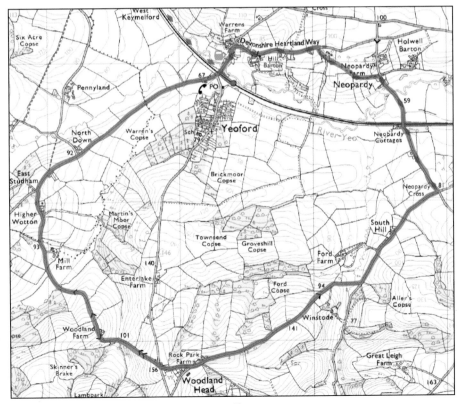

YEOFORD

Walk 2. Yeoford to Copplestone. 3.4 miles. 2.5 hours.
A varied walk along the lanes and footpaths of the mid-Devon redlands and through
the unspoilt hamlet of Coleford. Chosen by *The Independent* (Dec 2011) as one of the
U.K's "50 Best Winter Walks," it's a treat at *any* time of year. Ideal for children.
Facilities: Pubs in Yeoford, Coleford and Copplestone. Village stores in Copplestone.

Do not exit the platform, but walk to its north (Barnstaple) end and pass under the bridge to join a footpath running alongside the line. Note the bare expanse immediately west of the bridge on the far side of the tracks, once the site of a brick-based 35-lever signal box built high enough for the signalman to look across the road bridge. After 0.2 miles cross the river Troney on a narrow footbridge. Autumn can produce excellent blackberries, and there are views ahead of the little village of Colebrooke and its hilltop church. At a metal gate descend and cross a narrow lane where it passes over the river Cole. After heavy rains the river can flood the road, and care should be taken. Pass through the metal kissing gate across the lane and continue walking northbound alongside the railway track to a gate leading to a large meadow. Sheep (and rabbits!) are often to be found in this field and dogs should be under close control.

At the far end of the meadow stands a gate. Turn right into a quiet lane which fords the river and enters Penstone. The substantial farm, Penstone Barton on the right beyond the ford, in some years offers late season PYO raspberries. Follow the road as it turns left past the barton and through Penstone, turning left again at the far end of the hamlet. Pass under the iron railway bridge, noting that it formerly provided a crossing for two tracks, and recross the river Cole by a stone bridge. Immediately beyond this bridge on the left is Penstone Glade, a pleasant place to rest. Its southern wooded end marks Coleford Junction, the actual dividing point between the North Devon line and the track that once headed off to south-west Devon and north Cornwall. The lane turns right here, but continue straight ahead, along a footpath crossing the Okehampton line. *Exercise caution*: ballast trains from Dartmoor's Meldon quarry occasionally use this track, and there are summer Sunday passenger services.

After crossing the line follow the field hedge uphill, joining a road at the summit to enter Colebrooke village. The peaceful church of St. Andrew provides another good

Ford at Penstone Barton

resting place and lovely views. Its traditional Devon cobblestone path from the front gate to the south porch is one of the best in the county. Walk to the east end of the churchyard where a gate in the metal railings opens onto a narrow footpath, Drunkards' Lane. Turn right downhill through the church car-park and then left into a lane. Proceed downhill, recrossing the Okehampton railway line, and at the bottom of the hill, bear left and continue for 0.3 miles to Coleford, one of mid-Devon's most picturesque villages. Pause at the crossroads, once the main road between Crediton and Bow, noting Spencer's Cottage with its cobbled porch on the northwest corner of the intersection. (The 13th Century "New" Inn lies a stone's throw to your right just over the bridge.)

Proceed straight ahead for a further mile past Coplestone (retaining the earlier spelling) House to a T-junction. Turn right to reach a major intersection. The village stores, pub and the ancient incised stone from which the village takes its name, can be found on the far side of the road bridge ahead of you. As you face the traffic lights, Copplestone station lies 0.2 miles to your left [SP Barnstaple] beyond a second bridge over the railway. Cross at the lights and detour through a lych gate to avoid walking in the road. The station is clearly signed to your right a few yards beyond the second bridge.

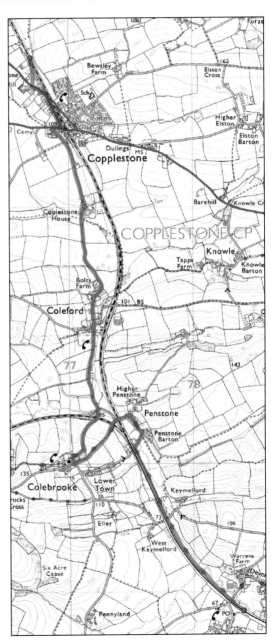

YEOFORD

Walk 3. Cenwahl & Culmin, Luke & Francis.
5.8 miles. 3.25 hours.
Through the Devon redlands to a forgotten battlefield.
Steep ascents are rewarded with lovely views.
Facilities: Pub at Yeoford. Library at Yeoford station.

Leave the station and turn right over the River Troney and past the pub. At the Yeoford Village intersection just beyond, bear right [SP Crediton & Exeter] and ascend a lane which has cut deeply into the red Permian sandstone soil. Follow this lane for 0.9 miles, keeping ahead at an unsigned crossroads to reach Marks Tree Cross. Bear right here and continue for a further 0.4 miles to Gunstone Cross. Turn right [SP Posbury] downhill, passing the entrances to Gunstone House and Dickers Farm to cross the railway and, immediately beyond, the River Yeo (whose waters merged with those of the Troney a few feet from the Yeoford station platform).

Neopardy from the River Yeo

At the sharp bend immediately beyond the river bridge, strike off to the left along a signed footpath which passes through the yard of Gunstone Mill and climbs along two field edges. Halfway up the hill the footpath merges with a (sometimes muddy) track, and the ascent continues. After 0.6 miles the track reaches a quiet lane, and the views begin in earnest. Ahead and far below, lies the peaceful Culvery valley. To your left along the road stands a distinctive grove of trees, the Posbury Clump, a well-known local landmark. The little chapel, also on your left and across the lane, was built in 1835 by a benefactor with the pleasing name of R. Hippisley Tuckfield and is dedicated to St. Luke.

Turn right along the lane for 150 yards to the point where a drive leads down to Posbury St. Francis. Once the home of the Tuckfields and, later, of the Hippisley family, it now houses a nunnery, the Community of the Franciscan Servants of Jesus and Mary, founded in 1934. (We'll be leaving the lane here but, if you're in no hurry and visibility is good, continue along the road for a few hundred yards and drink in the glorious view north across the Yeo valley.)

Just beyond the entrance to the Franciscan Community, where the lane bends right, ignore the footpath sign, but continue

ahead along an unsigned oak-bordered track (also offering spectacular views). After 0.2 miles at an intersection [Merrymeet] turn right, away from the bridleway, and continue for a further 0.5 miles along a second unsigned track. Above you on the right stands Castle Down, the site of an Iron Age fort and, later, an eastern outpost of the the ancient Celtic kingdom of Dumnonia. Historians consider it likely that this is the site of the battle of Posentesburh, fought in 661 A.D. between the Saxons, steadily expanding westwards from Dorset under their king, Cenwahl, and the Dumnonians led by their ruler, Culmin. The battle-hardened Saxons triumphed, driving Culmin off the fertile redland soil and west towards Cornwall.

Follow the track until it reaches a lane. Turn left passing Demmitts Linhay and continue to a T-junction [Blackdown Cross]. Here turn right, following the road downhill and taking time to enjoy the wonderful views. Colebrooke church is clearly visible. Just beyond Frankland Farm, at Norsworthy Grave, the road divides. Stay left [SP Yeoford] to reach Lower Neopardy Cross and continue ahead, recrossing railway and river, into Neopardy, little more than a cluster of houses on the hillside. Immediately beyond the wall-mounted letter box, turn left along a signed footpath. This initially follows an ancient way, carpeted with centuries of leaf mould, before heading clockwise around a large field to join a second track leading uphill to a road. Turn left and follow this road back to Yeoford.

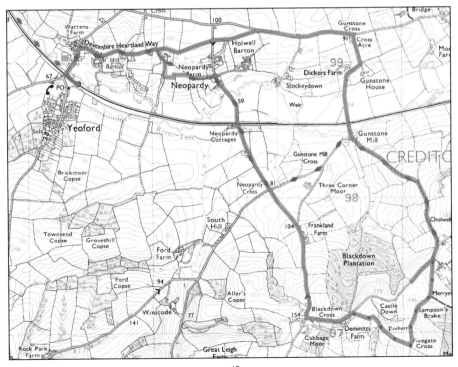

45

YEOFORD

Walk 4. Culm Clay & Permian Sandstone.
One-way to Copplestone. 4.6 miles. 2.75 hours.
A pleasant walk through the changing soils of mid-Devon.
Facilities: Pub at Yeoford; Library at Yeoford station.
Pub and village stores at Copplestone.

Leave the station and turn left over the railway bridge. If you glance over the left side of the bridge parapet, you'll see that two staircases once led down to the platforms, a reminder of the days when remote Yeoford was "Yeoford *Junction*," the last station before the tracks divided a mile further north along the line. One branch headed to Okehampton for onward service either to Tavistock and Plymouth, or Bude or Padstow. The other branch followed the route of today's Tarka Line to Barnstaple, with continuing service to Bideford, Torrington and Ilfracombe.

THE
DEVON
BELLE

SOUTHERN
RAILWAY

Southern Railway provided several corridor coach through-trains from London (Waterloo), among them the "Devon Belle" (complete with rear observation car) and the "Atlantic Coast Express," which became progressively smaller as it was divided and sub-divided depending on the coach's final destination. (Boarding the *correct* portion of the train in London was therefore vital!) A similar metamorphosis occurred in the reverse direction: Devon and Cornwall passengers boarding a two- or three-coach train at Lapford or Padstow found themselves, by Salisbury, part of a twelve-coach express!

Beyond the railway bridge bear right [SP Hittisleigh] and continue gently uphill for 0.7 miles to North Down Cross. Turn right [SP Colebrooke] downhill to the Troney River bridge. Ignoring a footpath sign just before the river, take the unsigned lane immediately *beyond* the bridge on the left. After 0.25 miles, turn right on a signed footpath leading along three field edges.

As you climb the first two field edges west of Pennyland (perhaps an early reference to the density of its soil) farm, note the immensely heavy "Culm Measures" earth, a *putty* coloured shale sandstone laden with clay. From the brow of the hill in the third field look ahead and to your left as you prepare to enter the distinctive *red* Permian sandstone of mid-Devon. Crossing the stile at the bottom of the third field, turn left and follow a lane, mostly uphill between (now red) earth banks. Ignoring all side turnings, a 0.3 mile walk brings you to the peaceful hilltop village of

Colebrooke. (The tile-capped cob wall to your left at the T-junction is clearly built of Permian sandstone, dispelling any doubts that you've now arrived in red-earth country.)

St. Andrew's Church has 12th Century origins and was enlarged several times. The lower stones of the tower are probably early 14th Century, the tower having been brought up to its present elevation 120 years or so later. Outside, the traditional Devon cobble paths are a delight, while the massive yew tree was planted as a seedling in 1795. Walk round to the far (north) side of the church to a railed path known as Drunkards' Lane. Turn left along the path and follow it to the church's west (tower) end and the village square.

Continue straight ahead across the square and along an unsigned track, which passes between cottages and behind a row of former Council houses before descending gently towards Brocks Farm. At a gate some 250 yards before the farm the path, rerouted in 2009, veers sharply right to follow the hedge down to the railway. (Having now separated from the North Devon "Tarka" Line, this branch leads to Okehampton and Meldon Quarry.) At the bottom of the field turn left and follow the railway for 300 yards to a narrow tunnel leading under the track and across a further field to reach a lane.

Turn right onto this peaceful lane, which immediately crosses a stream, and follow it uphill past the entrances to Butsford and Horwell Bartons for 0.7 miles to a hilltop crossroads [Broomhill Cross]. Continue ahead [SP Copplestone] for a further 0.8 miles to a row of thatched cottages. Immediately beyond them, take a signed footpath to your right over a stile and

across a field to another lane. Dog-leg 30 yards right across this lane to rejoin the footpath which skirts the Pope Garden allotments before meeting the main road at a railway bridge. Bear right over the bridge, and at the next road junction, by the ancient copple stone, turn sharp left against the one-way traffic flow to reach a second railway bridge. Cross this, noting Copplestone station platform to your right. The station approach road lies just beyond the bridge.

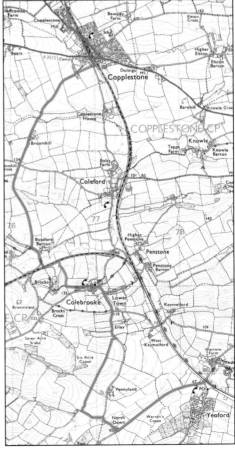

COPPLESTONE

Situated some 110 metres (360 ft) above sea level, Copplestone is both the highest point on the line and the peninsula watershed, all rivers to the South draining eventually into the Exe, and those to the North wending their way towards the Bristol Channel. The station also marked the furthest point from Exeter to which a double row of track was once provided. This twin track, laid in 1883, remained in operation for 88 years. Between 1871 and 1971 the surrounding population fell by some 45%, but has since increased with a number of new housing estates appearing in Copplestone since the start of this century. In its heyday the station sported cattlepens, a slaughterhouse at the northern end of the platform, and both five- and two-tonne cranes.

Walk 1. A Journey back through Time. 5.0 miles. 3 hours.
This walk through the mid-Devon redlands to the remote hamlet
of Newbuildings is entirely along local lanes and may be undertaken after rain. The walk
offers fine views and provides a fascinating glimpse of the Devon of 300 years ago.
Facilities: Pub and village stores in Copplestone.

Turn left outside the station and walk up to the main road. Turn left again and follow the Exeter-bound traffic over the bridge and towards the village centre. After 0.35 miles, just before the end of the one-way system and immediately beyond the Cross Hotel, turn left up Bewsley Hill past the primary school. As the road gains altitude, the views open up. To the South-west, the northern hills of Dartmoor -- the distinctive rounded shape of Cawsand (or Cosdon) Beacon, and to the right, the sharper outline of Yestor -- dominate the horizon. Three miles to the North, on its high ridge, Morchard Bishop church tower is clearly visible.

After 1.7 miles, prepare to step back in time as you enter the sleepy old hamlet of Newbuildings. Two centuries ago it was rather less sleepy, for the tiny main street lay on the old high road connecting Exeter and Crediton with Barnstaple, a busy goods and stagecoach route. Nowadays border collies lie lethargically in the road and soak up the summer sun. The building of the turnpike road in the valley in the early 19th Century, and the railway that was later constructed alongside it, put paid to the dreams, not only of Newbuildings, but of many another village along the old ridgeway.

From the Newbuildings Cross intersection, retrace your steps for a few yards back along the road to Copplestone before turning left and uphill along a narrow, unsigned lane. After 0.4 miles, Higher Woolsgrove farm comes into view. The farm offers an excellent opportunity to observe Devon cob walls in various states of health. Cob is a Devon speciality. A mixture of local red earth, water, manure and straw is applied in horizontal layers, and will last

for centuries provided it is accompanied by two essentials: a good "hat" and stout "boots". Its top must be protected from the elements by thatch, tile or slate, and its bottom by stone, or the entire wall quickly collapses into its original components. Beyond the farm, the road descends sharply to pass Woolsgrove farm (with another nice cob barn and the cluck of chickens). After briefly rising from the valley bottom, the lane ends at a T-junction [Woolsgrove Cross] 0.8 miles from Newbuildings.

Turn right here and, in 0.3 miles at Brandirons Corner, right again. Ahead lies Elston Barton, a magnificent Devon longhouse in a rare L-shaped configuration. Note the massive buttresses supporting the east wall. The front door is reached, unusually, through a courtyard around the bend on the north side of the property. At the unsigned road junction

just beyond, turn left past the post box and enjoy fine views as you stroll gently downhill. In 0.4 miles at the old Copplestone school "enlarged 1898", turn right along the A377 main road back to the village.

The Copple Stone

The copple stone from which the village takes its name stands at the first intersection. It ranks among the finest to be found in south-west England, despite the fact that the crosshead, which would originally have surmounted the incised granite shaft, is missing. Dating from the 10th Century, the stone was mentioned in the charter awarded to the village in 947A.D. Towards the end of the last century it was moved to its present position to facilitate traffic flow. Retrace your steps to the station at the northern (Barnstaple) end of the village.

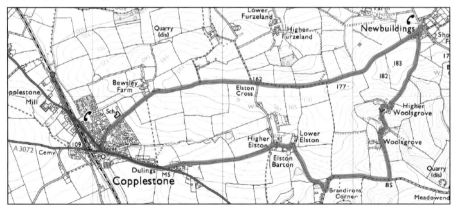

COPPLESTONE

Walk 2. One-way to Morchard Road Station. 5.5 miles. 3.5 hours.
This walk, like its predecessor, begins with a visit to the remote hamlet of Newbuildings,
before heading across even less travelled country to connect
with the next station down the line.
Facilities: Pub and village stores in Copplestone.
Pub and Public Conveniences at Morchard Road.

Turn left outside the station and left again at the main road. Follow the Exeter-bound traffic over the bridge and towards the centre of the village. Just before the end of the one-way system and immediately beyond the Cross Hotel, turn left up Bewsley Hill past the primary school.

After 1.7 miles enter the sleepy old hamlet of Newbuildings, an isolated settlement on the old main road between Barnstaple and Exeter. At the Newbuildings Cross intersection, turn left [SP Morchard Bishop]. Ignoring the first fork to the right after 0.4 miles, proceed along the old coaching road for a further 0.3 miles to a distinctive Scots Pine tree marking Gays Cross. Here take the left-hand fork [SP Gays & Knathorne].

This quiet country lane is a delight. Over the right hedge the tower of Morchard Bishop church stands out against the sky, while to the left lie the distant hills of Dartmoor: the distinctive rounded shape of Cawsand (or Cosdon) Beacon and further to the right, the

sharper outline of Yestor. The little lane passes Gays Farm, a square Georgian house with a fine old stone barn and, a little further along on the opposite side of the road, a track leads up to Bagborough, a splendid thatched Devon longhouse. Note the tall chimneys

The DEVON BELLE

	Waterloo	dep	5.20 pm
12.0 pm			
3.16 pm	Sidmouth Jct.	dep	2.3 pm
3.36 pm	Exeter Ctl.	dep	1.40 pm
5.32 pm	Ilfracombe	dep	12.0 noon
5.36 pm	Plymouth Friary	dep	11.30 am

NEW!

ALL-PULLMAN TRAIN TO THE WEST OF ENGLAND
with Observation Car
SOUTHERN RAILWAY & PULLMAN CAR COMPANY

to minimize the risk of fire. At Ash Bullayne the lane veers hard right and then left, later crossing Knathorne Brook to reach an often muddy crossroads where a footpath crosses the road by a large barn.

Turn left here and walk past the barn to a point just beyond it where the footpath divides. Turn sharp right and follow the edge

of a large field, with the hedge first on your right and later on your left, to reach a stile. Climb over and strike out diagonally across the hilltop to reach another stile in the opposite corner leading to steps down to a plantation. Turn left to reach Slade Farm, a modern structure whose ancient outbuildings (the original farm) may be glimpsed through a gateway on your left.

Here your route intersects with the Two Moors Way which runs due north/south at this point. Go through the small gate ahead of you and descend a few yards towards the pond to reach a way post. Bear right for about 50 yards to cross a stream on a gated footbridge. Head directly up the field on the far bank passing through concrete gateposts, then diagonally across the next field to a gate

by the Victorian front of Southcott. Follow the further field edge to reach a road.

Turn left downhill. The road levels out shortly before crossing Knighty Brook. Beyond on the right is an area where the Council have for more than half a century kept their equipment. (Steam traction engines were a common sight here in the 1940s and 1950s.) As you cross the bridge, note Morchard Road station a few hundred yards to your right. The similarity of the station's architecture to the buildings you left behind at Copplestone is striking.

At the busy main road, turn right and carefully make your way to the station approach road, which is on your right just opposite the turning to Winkleigh.

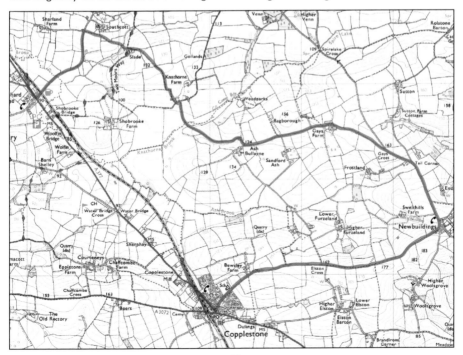

COPPLESTONE

Walk 3. One-way to Yeoford Station. 4.8 miles. 2.75 hours.
The initial bustle of traffic along the A377 gives
way to peaceful lanes and footpaths.
Facilities: Pub and village stores in Copplestone.
Pub at Yeoford. Library at Yeoford station.

Turn left outside the station and walk up to the main road, noting the ancient barn directly opposite. In recent years several new estates have been built in Copplestone. Although you can still see the occasional thatched cottage, most of the village housing is no earlier than 19th Century -- evidence of the commercial pressures the Exeter-Barnstaple Turnpike (1828-1831) and the railway (1854) exerted upon a once remote rural hamlet.

At the main road turn left and follow the Exeter-bound traffic over the railway bridge into the village. At the end of the one-way system stands the 10th Century (or earlier) copple stone from which the village takes its name. The derivation of the name *copple* is in some dispute. It has been argued that it derives from the Saxon word *copelan* meaning to move or rock (something, apart from a repositioning in the 1960s to accommodate traffic flow, the stone has

not done in recorded memory). Others note that *copple* simply means "to come to a point." (Since the top of the shaft -- and the cross piece -- are lost, this hypothesis must also be taken on trust!)

Continue ahead [SP Exeter] uphill along the main road. Your route, along what is now the A377, was first surveyed in 1826 by John Loudon McAdam, who was then employed by the Exeter Turnpike Trust. Road construction between Exeter and Barnstaple began two years later. For the only time along the entire 39-mile route the railway here forsakes the turnpike, looping south towards Colebrooke, whose church tower you can see, and Yeoford, before rejoining the A377 at Crediton.

At the end of the village by the old school bear left up a narrow lane. After 0.4 miles, just before a cob-walled red-roofed barn, turn right onto a signed footpath with lovely views of Dartmoor. Follow the path downhill along three field edges and past Amber Cottage (with its rounded bread oven) to rejoin the A377 at Barehill Farm. Turn left along the pavement for 150 yards until the lane to Knowle is directly opposite. Cross the A377 with *extreme care* and follow this lane (past another bread oven) for 0.3 miles to Knowle Barton's cob-walled barn. Beyond the barton and a wall-mounted letter box, turn left up a track marked "Unsuitable for Motors" past the farm's thatch-topped walls and ancient granite gateposts.

At the end of the track, at a T-junction, turn right, uphill, to reach Raddon Down Cross on what was, before 1831, the main road between Crediton and Bow. Proceed straight ahead [SP Yeoford]. American readers may recall that the refuse/recycling site at Moab, UT. is regularly voted the "most scenic" in the U.S.A. Punchbowl Recycling Center, 0.3 miles along this lane, is a worthy contender for the U.K. title.

There are often sheep here and dogs should be under control. At the meadow's far end, pass through a gate and continue alongside the line to a kissing gate and a lane. (Be careful here as the River Cole regularly floods.) Go through the gate on the lane's far side, and continue beside the track (blackberries available in season), over the River Troney and on to Yeoford Station.

Roughly 0.2 miles beyond Punchbowl, turn right at a signed footpath following the entrance road downhill to Southcoombe farm. The view is stunning with Colebrooke church tower again visible. Southcoombe has a wonderfully remote feel with its ancient sandstone barn, leaded windows and a tree (with a rope ladder) that must have given pleasure to generations of children. Continue along field edges just above the valley bottom, crossing the stream and aiming, after 0.5 miles, for a large pond. Shortly beyond, the path crosses an orchard and swings right to reach Penstone Barton, where late season PYO raspberries (and cider) are sometimes available. At the lane beyond the lovely old barton, turn left over an idylllic ford (a picturesque spot to consume surplus berries!) Just before the railway bridge beyond, turn left into a water meadow.

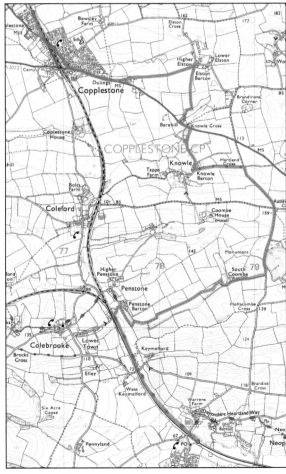

COPPLESTONE

Walk 4. The Three Hamlets: Elston, Knowle and Coleford.
4.5 miles. 3 hours.
There's a sense of "getting away from it all" about this gentle meander through the lanes and footpaths of mid-Devon's red earth country.
Facilities: Pub and village stores in Copplestone. Pub at Coleford.

Turn left outside the station and walk up to the main road. Turn left again and follow the Exeter-bound traffic over the bridge and towards the village centre. After 0.35 miles, at the end of the one-way system and immediately beyond the Cross Hotel, pause to admire the Saxon copple stone from which the village takes its name. It marks a boundary point common to three parishes: Crediton, Colebrooke and Down St. Mary. Turn left up Bewsley Hill past the school. The wall of the last house features an old bread oven, a reminder of the days when all baking was done at home. After 0.8 miles, just beyond an overgrown milk-churn stand on the left, turn right [SP Elston Cottages] along a lane offering glorious views.

After 0.2 miles, by an enormous cob-walled barn (note the protruding wooden cross beams) turn left past Elston Barton, a superb Devon longhouse with an unusual rear cobbled courtyard. The lane skirts the barton before continuing past its pond to a T-junction [Brandirons Corner]. Turn right [SP Crediton] and after 150 yards take a signed footpath to the right. This path leads past poultry houses,

beyond the last of these ducking left to a stile (and, in 2012, a fine old stone roller), then across a field to reach a thatched cottage by the A377.

Mid-Devon's distinctive Permian sandstone soil

© Sally Discombe

Built between 1828 and 1831 by a consortium headed by the Earl of Portsmouth, this turnpike road (and the railway which followed in 1854) revolutionised local transportation. Cross the main road with *extreme care*, for traffic is fast and visibility poor, making for the lane [SP Knowle] directly opposite. This lane leads past Stowford Cottage, a fine thatched longhouse (with another bread oven), to reach the tiny hamlet 0.3 miles ahead. Knowle Barton retains its bell tower -- harking back to the days when the field labourers could be summoned by the toll of the farm bell -- and

the tiny community even has its own church dedicated to St. Boniface (no surprise when you consider that Crediton is barely three miles distant). At one time, Knowle also had the distinction of having its own quarry at Bitter Knowle, a nearby farm long since reverted to the red earth. Stone from this quarry was used to repair Colebrooke church tower in the late 17th Century.

When, just beyond the church, the lane bends left, stay ahead along a signed footpath (more of a farm track) which passes Knowle Farm, its cob wall protected by a thatched "hat", and several other farms before becoming a peaceful, and obviously ancient, green way with a wonderful air of timelessness. Reverting to a footpath leap-frogging beside hedges, the route passes through a little wood and, amazingly, a substantial and beautifully engineered arch under the railway. Follow the path across a final field to a stile (and an old iron gate) opening onto a lane.

Before the opening of the Earl's turnpike in 1831, this lane -- the original main road from Crediton to Bow -- was a route of some importance, achieving turnpike status and with its own toll houses. Only after the opening of the new turnpike did Coleford revert to comparative obscurity. By the 1850s the railway surveyors who had gone to the expense of providing that costly bridge deemed Coleford undeserving even of a halt for, by then, the smart commercial money was on Copplestone.

Turn right down the hill (with Colebrooke church on the horizon) past the thatched pub

and over the River Cole, a peaceful little stream ... but not always. In November 1841, the same torrential rains that brought tragedy to a local curate [See Morchard Road: Walk 4] caused devastation here. "In the little village of Coleford a melancholy and distressing spectacle meets the eye, no less than seven or eight buildings being entirely destroyed, comprising the property of humble industrious individuals, who have, by this unfortunate event, been deprived of their little all."

Two centuries earlier, in July 1644, the hamlet witnessed another major event, when Charles I reviewed his troops from the cobbled porch of Spencer's Cottage just ahead at the village crossroads. Turn right here along a lane which later passes Coplestone House (note the old spelling), for centuries the home of the Coplestone family, their great antiquity celebrated in the old adage: "Crocker, Cruwys and Coplestone, when the Conqueror came were all at home." At the T-junction 0.4 miles beyond, bear right at the traffic lights and cross over the bridge to the copple stone. Retrace your steps to the station.

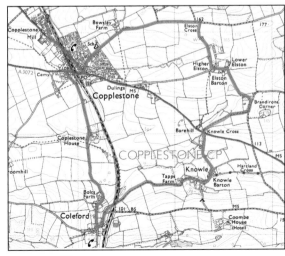

COPPLESTONE

Walk 5. One-way to Yeoford via the Two Moors Way.
5.9 miles. 3.5 hours.

An opportunity to sample the Two Moors Way as it winds through the rich red fields of mid-Devon. Spectacular views beyond Brock's Cross.

Facilities: Pub and village stores in Copplestone. Pub at Yeoford. Library at Yeoford station.

Turn left outside the station and walk up to the main road. Turn left again but remain on the west side of the track, walking *against* the one-way Barnstaple-bound flow of vehicles. Where the pavement ends, a pedestrian diversion through a housing estate (bear left to exit via the lych gate) brings you to traffic lights. Cross and take the signed footpath immediately before the railway bridge. (Several walks in this book discuss the village's famous copple stone. If you're not familiar with it, divert a few yards left across the bridge and refer to the text.)

The footpath skirts allotments to emerge at a lane. Dog-leg 30 yards right and rejoin the path on the lane's far side. Cross the next field aiming just right of the cottages. A stile gives access to a quiet road. Turn left, later crossing a stream at a gauging station before climbing past a farm to Broomhill Cross. Pause here for a moment and look left. An electric cable strung on tall poles accompanies the road to Coleford. Both the second and third poles from the intersection have four (unused) horizontal wooden cross pieces mounted with insulators -- a rarity today, but a familiar sight until the late 20th Century, when poles like these carried a mass of telephone wires and could be found alongside almost every road and railway line in the country.

Turn right [SP Bow] onto the old turnpike between Bow and Crediton, and walk downhill between high banks of red Permian sandstone. At the bottom of the hill two Victorian gateposts guard the entrance to Paschoe House and Dairy Farm (which we'll later be passing). Across the road a utilitarian brick structure marks the Coleford Bore Hole. (That it ever secured planning permission is remarkable. The building's single redeeming feature is the fact that its brick exterior blends into the magnificent sandstone earth that now surrounds you on all sides.) Ahead among the trees on the skyline you can detect the tower of Clannaborough church.

Continue ahead for 0.8 miles past two mysterious stone gateposts on the right, all that remains of a (now ploughed under) drive to Clannaborough. Cross a stream before gradually ascending to Appledore Farm's concrete entrance drive, once a section of the Two Moors Way. Health & Safety, ever vigilant, have decreed that we must now walk 50 yards further west to a signed footpath on the left. In summer months this remote spot presides over a remarkable amount of pedestrian traffic, for this is the intersection of the Two Moors Way and the 45-mile long Devonshire Heartland Way linking Stoke Canon with Okehampton. (There's some guilty pleasure to be derived from the fact that your back-pack is feather-light in comparison with some of the ones you're likely to encounter during the next mile or so!)

The footpath deposits you just beyond the farm where a track leads up the wooded hillside. About 200 yards beyond the brow, the path turns left and follows a field edge down

HIKE for HEALTH
SOUTHERN RAILWAY
Go-as-you-please cheap tickets
get you to the country quickest
Ask for details at any S·R·Office and buy
'Southern Rambles' by S·P·B·Mais 6d

DEVON (SR)

to Paschoe Dairy Farm, newly rebuilt with a nice clock tower and weathervane. Turn right through a gate, shortly passing below Paschoe House (rebuilt 1852 in neo-Tudor style). For more than three centuries the home of the Hamlyn family, it may have been here that "Uncle" Tom Cobley signed his will in 1787.

The footpath continues along the west bank of a stream. When it divides (the Two Moors Way branching right) *keep left* above the water along a lovely hedge of beech trees whose nuts, accumulating over decades, make for wonderfully soft walking. After dog-legging 20 yards left across a lane, continue along three field edges to Horwell Barton. Turn left up the barton's entrance drive to reach a road. Turn right (Colebrooke church tower monitors your progress) down to a stream and follow the road uphill to Butsford Bridge Cross. Turn left over the railway and renew your climb to Brock's Cross. Continue ahead on an unmetalled right of way offering superb views in all directions. At

Elley Cross keep ahead and downhill to reach a railway bridge, where after heavy rains the lane may flood. Immediately beyond the railway a metal gate on the right gives access to a footpath that parallels the track to Yeoford station 0.4 miles distant.

Awaiting your train at Yeoford, pause by the farther station bench, where a plaque commemorates Leonard "Lenny" Gillard, a Colebrooke farmer with no car and a lifelong love of the railway. On the afternoon of his funeral at St. Andrew's church in March 2005, the 13:52 from Barnstaple, passing below in the valley, sounded a long strident note on its whistle to bid him farewell.

MORCHARD ROAD

As its name implies, Morchard Road station is located some distance from the village of Morchard Bishop. Despite this, its passenger figures in the early 1900s always exceeded those of Copplestone. The architecture and original layout of the two stations were very similar.

Walk 1. Morchard Bishop. 5.9 miles. 4 hours

This walk gives a feel for what a rail passenger, too poor to take the pony trap, and unable to hitch a ride with the carrier, was once required to do: "walk up from the station." The route utilises several footpaths, the outbound section joining the Two Moors Way. A joy in fine weather, the paths are harder going after rain, the section before Gollands being spectacularly muddy. Select appropriate footwear!

Facilities: Pub & Toilets at Morchard Rd. Pub (closed Mon lunch) & stores at Morchard Bishop.

Turn left at the end of the station approach onto the A377. Exercise care. Beyond the pub turn left [SP Morchard Bishop] over the railway bridge. In 0.6 miles, opposite the entrance to Sharland Farm, turn right through a gate onto a path leading along a field edge. You're heading for Slade (the white house across the valley). At Southcott farm, the footpath enters a field. Walk diagonally across to the concrete gateposts and down the field beyond to reach a gated footbridge some 50 yards left of Slade. Cross this bridge and bear right up to another gate by the farm entrance.

On this gate's far side, turn left to join the Two Moors Way as it forges north across fields and up an ancient way to Weeke. Here, dog-leg right across the road onto a grassy track leading past farm buildings to Woodgate. The iron gate across the path beyond was made around 1900 at Webber Bros' Morchard Bishop smithy, still (2012) in operation. The path subsequently divides. Keep left, aiming for the upper part of the village. (Interested in seeing where the gate originated? Take the *right-hand* fork to Frost. The Webbers' forge is just across the intersection. Then walk uphill to the village centre.)

Morchard has Saxon origins, its name being derived from *Mor-ced*: Great Wood. Two centuries ago the village was twice as large, its London Inn a staging post on the Barnstaple - Exeter high road. The coming of the valley turnpike in 1831-- offering the horse-drawn coaches a better road, no hills and faster journey times -- left Morchard remote and isolated until cars became commonplace after World War II. Beyond the war memorial, the village boasts the longest continuous row of thatched cottages in the county. (The row would have been even longer were it not for a thatch fire in August 1907 which demolished the two properties at the top.)

From the road junction by the pub, follow Church Street for 0.25 miles to St. Mary's Church. The school across the road briefly educated Ernest Bevin, a Labour party minister who could scarcely have had a more disadvantaged beginning. The child of a single mother, he was orphaned at the age of nine, yet went on to found the TGWU (1922) and was a key member of the World War II coalition government. (Readers interested in Bevin may like to know that the house in which he lived as a child is situated

on the A377 just across from the former Copplestone Mills.) Morchard Bishop had its share of evacuees from the London blitz. The city children, not always receiving a friendly welcome from the locals, were permitted to leave school ahead of their rural peers to avoid being pelted with clods of earth!

Enter the churchyard with its lovely view of Dartmoor. St Mary's tower can be seen for miles around, and in 1952 sustained a meteorite strike. Leave by the east gate to enter a shady glebe. Haytor Rocks can be spotted on the southern skyline and, directly beneath them, the tower of Colebrooke church. Pass through the further glebe gate, turn right and descend steeply. At the next junction continue downhill. When the lane merges with the old high road to Newbuildings, bear left and continue for 0.2 miles, passing Oldborough Cross. Just beyond Higher Oldborough, look on the right for a stile and signposted footpath leading diagonally across two fields. At the bottom of the second field the path joins Gollands Lane, something of a quagmire.

Growing up near Morchard in the 1940s, I was told of three lanes famed for their horrific conditions and going by the splendid names of Mucksypot, Gooseypool and Featherbed. Alas, I never learnt their precise locations, but what is now innocuously known as Gollands Lane could well have been one of the three.

Spare a thought then for the schoolchildren of the 1920s who daily trudged up from Knathorne Farm, which you'll later pass, only to face the school-master's wrath at their encrusted boots. Descend left into the lane (for which you may soon have a name of your own!) and follow the childrens' ghosts for 0.4 miles, down and then up past Gollands (where the track improves) to their old home at Knathorne. Shortly beyond this farm a muddy crossroads is dominated by a large barn. Proceed ahead keeping the barn immediately on your right to a point just beyond where the footpath divides. Turn right and follow the field edge, the hedge first on your right and later on your left, to reach a stile. Climb this, striking out diagonally across the hilltop to reach another stile in the opposite corner with steps down to a plantation. Turn left to Slade Farm and retrace your route to the station.

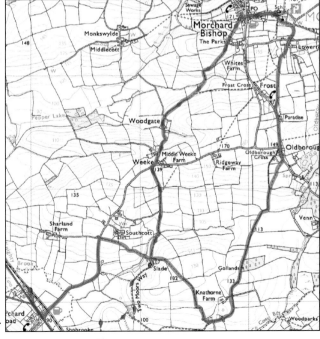

MORCHARD ROAD

Walk 2. The Parish of Down St. Mary. 4.7 miles. 4 hours.
This walk, along footpaths for virtually its entire length, can be muddy. Take appropriate footwear. Control dogs near livestock and shut all gates (there are lots; it's worth keeping count). Navigation is a bit challenging; keep a close eye on the map!
Facilities: Pubs at Morchard Road and, just off the route, at Zeal Monachorum.

On leaving the station cross the A377 and take the B3220 [SP Winkleigh]. After 0.25 miles a footpath crosses the road. Turn left onto Ellicombe Farm's drive. Bear right and advance almost to the farm before taking a signed gate on the left giving access to a field. Walk over the hill, descend and pass through a second gate. Turn sharp right for a few yards passing through a third metal gate, and then left into a muddy field. Forge uphill to reach a metal gate at the top of the coomb. Pass through and turn left to reach a final gate opening into a lane.

Turn left along the lane. After 150 yards watch for a stile and footpath sign in the right-hand hedge. Take this path across the first field and then bear left over more stiles. Immediately beyond one of them keep a sharp lookout for a footpath fork, one route leading ahead to a wooden shed and a second veering right. *Turn right here*, crossing several fields to reach Middle Yeo Farm, where the footpath meets a metalled farm lane. Turn left past the misleadingly named "old farm" to reach a road.

Turn right. At the bottom of the hill, leave the road where it bends right just before the bridge and, remaining on the *same side* of the river, take the signed footpath and follow the east bank of the River Yeo upstream for 0.6 miles. On the far side of the wood, ignore the footbridge but continue ahead to Tuckingmill Bridge, just beyond a disused quarry. The pub lies across the bridge and uphill on the right.

Tuckingmill Bridge is a tranquil spot, but 200 years ago it would have been bustling. The quarry and the tucking mill just ahead rivalled farming as major village industries, and account for so sturdy a bridge in the middle of nowhere. Tucker is a common Devon surname deriving from the process used by the early woollen industry to "tuck" or "full" (hence the surname Fuller) woven cloth by pounding it with water driven hammers or "stocks." The natural oil that protected the sheep from Devon downpours was removed with "fuller's earth," a clay with detergent properties.

Continue upstream with the river to your right, noting the ruined mill and the leat that provided water to power the wheel. A few yards beyond, to the left of a cottage, the path divides. Take the left fork along a track bordering the trees before ducking into a bluebell wood at a stile. Emerging from the trees the path crosses a large field to reach another stile. In the field beyond, keep the hedge on your right before crossing to its other side at a stile opposite Oak Tree Farm. With the hedge now on your left, aim for the entrance to a third field, where a stream and footpath cross at right-angles. Proceed ahead and uphill to a gate leading into a lane.

Cross the lane and, just to the right of Merrifield Farm drive, take the footpath leading across a large field. At the far side, beyond a metal gate, is a footpath crossroads. Turn sharp left here, passing through a second gate to follow the upper field edge

HIKE for HEALTH
SOUTHERN RAILWAY
Go-as-you-please cheap tickets
get you to the country quickest
Ask for details at any S.R Office and buy
"Southern Rambles" by S·P·B·Mais 6d

DEVON (SR)

for 0.2 miles. A stream on your right parallels the path. At the field's far end descend to the water where it joins a second stream coming down from the hill above and to your right. Cross the newly united waters on a footbridge and turn right, the path following first the "new" stream uphill and later two field edges. At the top of the last field, from which three church towers are visible, a gate leads to a lane by Lower Thorne Farm.

Dog-leg left into the lane, watching for a poorly positioned footpath sign ten yards along in the right-hand hedge. Take the footpath past farm outbuildings to a field, often containing horses. A pond lies below and to your left. Continue across the field to reach a wood where a stream is crossed by railway sleepers. Note the badger setts. (The word "set" has more explanatory text than any other entry in the OED!) In spring this little wood is ablaze with primroses. Cross the stream and bear left downhill through

the wood to reach a field with a stile. Head over this and up a final field aiming just left of a thatched cottage. At the cottage turn left onto a sometimes muddy bridleway. When the bridleway finally meets a lane, bear right and uphill to Down St. Mary. Why *uphill*? Intriguingly, the Anglo-Saxon word from which *down* is derived meant *hill-top*. St. Mary's church has 12th Century origins. Note the mediaeval pew ends, and the unusual 19th Century swivelling lych gate that doubles as a coffin rest.

From the church, take the lane [SP Morchard Road] past the village pump and granite trough. Once the village is behind you, watch for a signed footpath in the left-hand hedge. Take this across a single field back to Ellicombe Farm and, when you reach it, turn right through a familiar gate into the hilly meadow separating the farm from Ellicombe House. Retrace your steps to the station.

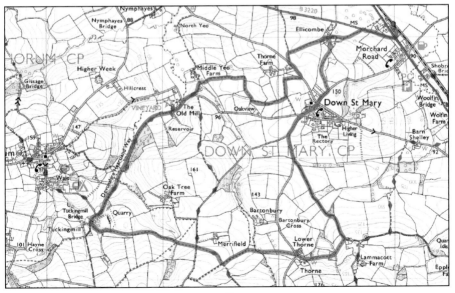

MORCHARD ROAD

Walk 3. One-way to Copplestone 3.3 miles. 2.5 hours
A comparatively short walk, suitable for older children,
though muddy after rain.
Facilities: Pub and public conveniences at Morchard Road.
Pub and village stores at Copplestone.

At the end of the station approach, turn left and carefully make your way along the busy A377. Beyond the pub, turn right [SP Down St. Mary] and head up Union Hill for 0.5 miles to the village.

The Church of St. Mary the Virgin, to your right, retains traces of its Saxon origins, as evidenced by the bas relief of Daniel in the lions' den above the Norman south door. The original Norman tower was rebuilt in 1413, and again (along with most of the church) in the late 19th Century. The pews, which thankfully survived this Victorian make-over, date from 1520 and may be from Simon Warman's Taunton workshop.

As you leave the church, note that the level of the churchyard is somewhat higher than the lane outside. This may indicate the churchyard's antiquity, its surface gradually rising over the centuries as its occupants increased in number.

At the village green turn left along a lane (unsigned by the fingerpost) to Higher Living Farm at the far end of the village. (Note that its substantial 19th Century barn, now

converted, retains its cruciform ventilation slits). At the bottom of the hill, opposite a row of oak trees, there's a footpath sign on your right. (This is the Two Moors Way, an 89-mile cross-county route between Ivybridge, south of Dartmoor, and Lynmouth, north of Exmoor. Opened with much fanfair in 1976, the Way is simply an agglomeration of ancient Devon footpaths. The paths which now comprise the

The path to Chaffcombe

Two Moors Way provided a useful route for peddlars, sailors and others to make their way between the English and the Bristol Channels.) Take this well-signed path for 0.4 miles through a pleasant oak grove, over a stream and through a wood, to a wayside T-junction at the top of a large field.

The Two Moors Way heads right here, but your route lies to the *left* along an unsigned bridleway (narrowing in places to a footpath) past fields, through a wood and over a stream to reach a metalled lane at a sharp corner.

This is Chaffcombe, a tiny farming settlement. The hamlet has the air of being buried in the remote past despite its proximity to Copplestone with its 19th Century turnpike road (the A377) and railway. At the corner, continue straight ahead for 0.2 miles to the bottom of the hill, where the lane crosses a stream. Just beyond, look for a stile and footpath sign half hidden in the right-hand hedge. Take this path up to Chaffcombe Farm. Once level with the farm, turn left through a stile and follow the upper edge of a field to a gate where the path divides. Continue ahead in the same direction (but with the hedge now on your left) along field edges to arrive at a main road (A3072). Turn left into the road and make your way carefully down to the traffic lights. Continue straight ahead over the railway bridge to the centre of Copplestone, where an incised stone presides over a road junction. This is the "copple stone" from which the village takes its name. The ten foot (3.2 metres)

high granite stone is among the finest late-Saxon artifacts of this type remaining in Southern England. It is certainly no later than mid-10th Century, since references both to a "copleston" and to the charter granted to the village in 947 A.D. appear in one of the *Anglo Saxon Chronicles*. Five other Devon cross shafts of similar date may be seen at Exeter Museum, Chulmleigh, Colyton, Dolton and Sidbury. At the stone, turn left against the one-way traffic flow, up the main street and over the railway bridge, noting the station's location to your right. The signed station approach lies a few yards beyond the bridge.

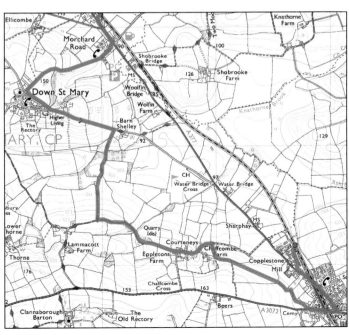

MORCHARD ROAD

Walk 4. The Melancholy Affair at Hayne Bridge 6.9 miles. 4 hours
A peaceful walk along lanes and footpaths to the site of a Victorian tragedy.
Facilities: Pubs at Morchard Road and Zeal Monachorum.
Public Conveniences at Morchard Road. Farm shop at Clannaborough.

At the end of the station approach, turn left and carefully make your way along the busy A377. Just beyond the pub, turn right [SP Down St Mary] and head uphill 0.5 miles to the village. Beyond St. Mary's church keep right [SP Zeal Monachorum] and 100 yards later bear right again along a lane which undulates down to the River Yeo. On the far side of the river bridge the lane veers left and then uphill. Towards the top be alert for a footpath sign in the left hedge, and follow this path uphill along five field edges. At the final stile dog-leg right for 30 yards

St. Peter's churchyard, Zeal Monachorum

before turning left into Zeal Monachorum, "the cell of the monks." The manor of "sele" was gifted to Buckfast Abbey in the 11th Century by tide-defying King Canute. St. Peter's churchyard with its ancient yew tree makes an excellent place for a rest.

Leave the village by the road to the South [SP Bow] which descends steeply. The large, non-traditional pub is just off this road to the left. Towards the bottom of the hill, at Hayne

Cross, continue ahead [SP Bow] to cross the River Yeo at Hayne Bridge. On the afternoon of 29th November, 1841, after days of heavy rain the curate of nearby Clannaborough, the Revd. H.A. Hughes, and his wife Sophia, 56, were returning by phaeton from a christening at Bondleigh, accompanied by one of their nine children, 18 year-old George on horseback, and Knowles their 15 year-old servant. Attempting to cross the swollen river, the entire party were swept into the waters with disastrous results. Mother, son and servant were drowned, and the curate, clinging to an overhanging alder bush 300 yards downstream, owed his life solely to "the cool judgement and intrepidity of Mr. Bibbings, of Zeal."

Continue up the hill beyond. At the first road junction, Clapper Cross (after another bridge, upstream and more ancient, but alas no longer extant) turn left [SP Copplestone] and follow the lane uphill to a ridge blessed with glorious views. After 1.7 miles, at the

second intersection, turn right to reach the Clannaborough Cross T-junction. Cross the main road with care to join a bridleway directly opposite. Once through the hedge turn left, briefly walking parallel with the road, until the way heads right across the field. After 200 yards, turn left along a track [The Two Moors Way] leading to a large beef and swede farm. This is Clannaborough. No village, just a church -- St. Petrock's -- where the unfortunate Mr. Hughes served as curate. A memorial to his wife and son may be seen on the south wall of the chancel, still candlelit in the evenings.

Follow the farm's entrance drive (past the farm shop) back to the main road. Turn right, keeping to the safety of a wide grass verge

for 200 yards. When you spot a *cul de sac* lane on the far (north) side of the road, cross with care and follow this lane for 0.2 miles to reach Lammacott Farm. Shortly beyond, the lane meets an isolated T-junction. Here forsake the Two Moors Way and head left past thatched Cheriton Cottage along the often muddy but delightfully named Cockrattle Lane. (*Not* as uncommon as you might think. There's another Cockrattle Lane only three miles north.) The lane leads down to a road. Here bear right uphill to Down St Mary. The church has very fine mediaeval carved pews, and an unusual 19th Century pivoting lych gate that doubles as a coffin rest. Beyond the church retrace your steps down Union Hill to the A377 crossroads and the railway station.

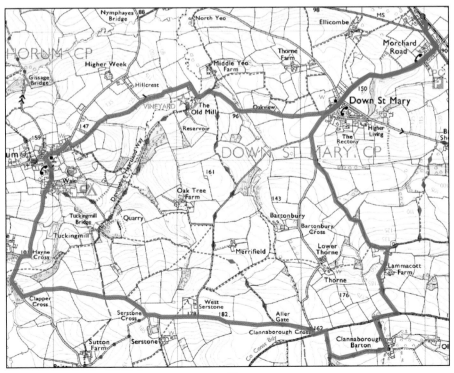

LAPFORD

Unlike its hilltop neighbour Morchard Bishop, Lapford's location on the lower slopes of the Yeo valley protected it from vicissitude. The arrival of the turnpike around 1830, and of the railway 25 years later, did not so much spell the doom of the village as place it firmly on the map. In the century prior to 1971 population remained stable, and from 1928 to 1970 the Ambrosia creamery provided a boost to the village economy, offering employment to local women and freight opportunities for the railway.

Walk 1. Coldridge, the Taw Valley & Nymet Rowland.
6.2 miles. 4 hours.

This walk -- part footpath, part country lanes -- includes an attractive section above the River Taw, and (if you're working your way northwards from Exeter) marks our first excursion into Henry Williamson's Tarka territory: "the Country of the Two Rivers."
Facilities: Pub (evenings only Mon-Thurs) and stores at Lapford.

Leave the station and turn right. Take extreme care as you edge along the busy A377 over the railway bridge. Just beyond the entrance to the old Ambrosia creamery, now a removals company, double back along a lane on the right [SP Nymet Rowland]. After 0.6 miles, at a T-junction, turn right and look for a footpath sign in the left hedge. As you follow this footpath along the hedgerow Coldridge church is visible ahead, Nymet Rowland church tower is to your right, and to your left lies the Dartmoor skyline. Dog-leg left across a lane and continue along the further field edge and over a marshy section to reach Coldridge Brook. Cross this on a gated footbridge and follow the footpath up the hill past a wood to reach Coldridge.

The stile at the village entrance offers fine views back over the route you have taken. Nymet Rowland, Lapford and, in the distance, Morchard Bishop church towers are visible. St. Mary's church in Coldridge is well worth a visit. The Norman font, with its seven flat arches decorating the top of each side, is exceptionally fine, and there are ancient pews in both aisles and in the Lady Chapel. The rood screen approaches that of Lapford for quality, and may well be the work of the same craftsmen.

Keep right at Coldridge village green, and at the next road junction [New Village Cross] bear right to take an unsigned lane leading downhill. After 0.2 miles watch on the left for the entrance to Mount Evelyn where a bridlepath intersects the lane. Turn left and immediately through a gate to enter a field, where the path (more *foot*path than bridle!) leads across several fields. At the entrance to the second field, note the flourishing badger setts above the stream to your right. On reaching the corrugated-iron barn, avoid the lane leading uphill, but bear slightly right along the lower contours of the water meadow to reach a gate opening onto a road. Turn right and cross the River Taw.

Just beyond the bridge, turn right onto a footpath, the Tarka Trail, which meanders above the western bank of the Taw past ruined Wood Farm. Coldridge church tower monitors your progress. Continue through Great and Burrowcleave woods -- radiant in springtime with bluebell and wood anemone -- to reach a lane 1.2 miles from the bridge where you joined the Tarka Trail. Follow this lane ahead and steeply uphill to Park Mill Crossroads, and here turn right [SP Nymet Rowland & Lapford]. Continue for 1.2 miles, descending once more to the river, crossed by a parapet-less bridge, and uphill again to Nymet Rowland. The 15th Century church of St. Bartholomew contains in the north aisle an ancient oak arcade dating from the same period -- one of only two to be found in Devon.

Walk the length of the village [SP Lapford] and, when the lane finally bends right, continue ahead along a footpath to Parsonage Farm and down through several fields to the railway and the River Yeo. Follow the footpath alongside the line past a further field before crossing the track by a bridge.

(From here, the former track layout at Lapford can be observed. A passing loop began well

beyond the A377 road bridge and ended at a set of points at the near end of the surviving "up" platform. Ambrosia's sidings lay to the right. The now defunct "down" platform was inconveniently sited on an isolated island in the middle of the loop, just beyond the

Lapford's lost "down" platform

A377 bridge from which it was reached by a staircase. Passengers from Waterloo or Exeter would alight on this island platform, lug their cases up the steps and confront whatever road traffic happened to be passing -- potentially lethal on winter nights!)

After crossing the bridge, continue along the far side of the track towards the station. The footpath passes just above an assembly area for agricultural equipment and then continues to the station entrance.

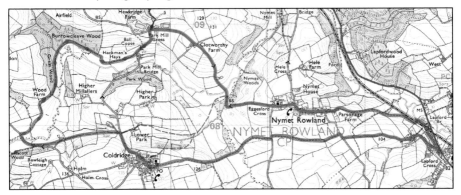

LAPFORD

Walk 2. Filleigh & Eastington. 4.5 miles. 3 hours.
After a stiff climb up from the River Yeo, this walk offers glorious views as it
follows quiet footpaths to the isolated hamlet of Filleigh. The return
route follows the north-west side of the Dalch valley.
Facilities: Pub (evenings only Mon-Thurs) and stores at Lapford.

Leave the station and turn left onto the busy A377 main road immediately crossing the River Yeo. Take particular care of children. There is no protection for pedestrians, who should walk along the far side of the road, facing the oncoming traffic from Barnstaple. (If you're unencumbered by children or dogs, note the plaque: "Lapford Bridge, erected Anno 1830 at the expense of the Trustees of the Exeter Turnpikes" and walk a few extra paces towards Barnstaple to admire the old milestone set in the hedge on the same side.) Several yards beyond the river bridge, turn right, uphill, along a signed footpath that leads to the village. The path joins the main street at a bend. Continue uphill to the village centre.

The ascent provides an excuse to stop and rest at the church -- dedicated to St. Thomas of Canterbury -- half-way up the hill. The

Lapford's St. Thomas of Canterbury church

building dates from the 12th Century, and may well have been constructed by William de Tracey, one of the four knights who murdered Thomas a Beckett, as penance for his deed. The interior is reached by an ancient door. The carved bench ends are 15th Century. The rood screen, dating from the early 16th Century, is one of the finest in the West Country.

Devotees of the macabre may like to know that a 19th Century Lapford rector, John Arundel Radford, was accused of murdering his curate. He escaped the gallows after being acquitted by a jury consisting mostly of his parishoners "who'd never hanged a parson yet, and weren't 'bout to start now!" Radford duly returned to his altar and pulpit for several more years until his death in May, 1867. His last wish, to be buried in the chancel, was refused by the authorities, and his grave lies just outside the door to the vestry. Legends have naturally accompanied this bit of local scandal, and there are apparently signs that the rector does not rest peacefully: the cross at his head (along with many others in the churchyard!) has a

stubborn tendency to list; a hole in his grave requires constant filling in; and Radford's ghost has been seen prowling the village by night.

A few steps beyond the church, at Orchard Cross, take the right-hand fork [SP Morchard Bishop & Eastington]. Continue uphill taking the second turning left (Park Meadow Close), at the top of which a stile gives access to a footpath. Follow this path diagonally across three fields to reach a drive leading around the back of Parsonage Farm. Here, at a footpath crossing, continue ahead through the gate and uphill, diagonally crossing four more fields to reach a lane. Dog-leg 20 yards left across this lane and follow first a drive and later a footpath around the lower perimeter of Great

Hole Farm. The footpath continues across fields, briefly through a coppice and up a farm track to reach a quiet lane. Turn right and follow the lane for 200 yards to Lower Filleigh Farm. From this corner, glance up the road to Filleigh Barton, the Georgian farmhouse that presides over the little community.

Take the signed footpath leading right from the corner, through Lower Filleigh farm (note the lovely wooden barn) and then along a track, field edges, and a further track. Descending to the valley, the track ends at a lane. Turn right past Cobley Farm. The River Dalch (pronounced *dolsh*) -- 200 yards or so to your left -- is also headed for Lapford. After 0.4 miles, the undulating lane passes

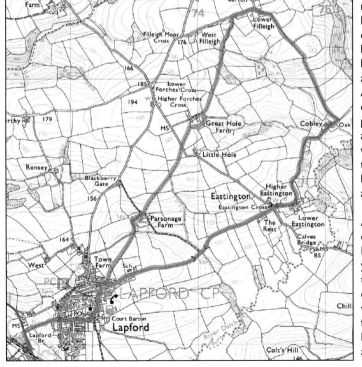

a gallop on the right and Lower Eastington Farm on the left. Just beyond, a fine cob barn is, sadly, being allowed to decay. At the Eastington crossroads, proceed straight ahead over what was, prior to 1831, the main road between Exeter and Barnstaple.

After a mile, on returning to Lapford, retrace your steps downhill through the centre of the village to the footpath leading back to the A377 and the station.

69

LAPFORD

Walk 3. A spot of ancient history. One-way to Morchard Road.
4.6 miles. 2.5 hours.
Apart from a muddy section between Lapford and Bury Barton,
the walk follows quiet lanes.
Facilities: Pub (evenings only Mon-Thurs) and stores at Lapford.
Pub & public conveniences at Morchard Road.

Pause at the main road immediately outside the station, noting the bridges to your right and left. Take care; the A377 offers no protection for pedestrians. If traffic is light and you're unaccompanied by children or dogs, cast your eye along the granite capstones topping the opposite (east) parapet of the railway bridge to your right. Spot the odd man out: a *concrete* slab above more recent brickwork, indicating where, from 1873 for almost a century, a wooden staircase led from the bridge to the "down" platform, an isolated island between the tracks. The river bridge over the Yeo, to your left, was custom-built in 1830 for the new turnpike.

Carefully walk a few yards further left, facing the oncoming traffic, before taking a signed footpath on the right leading up to the village. Follow Lapford's main street uphill but, after the road bends left at Court Barton, take a signed footpath leading to the right along a track and down to a stile. The footpath then follows a field edge before ducking under the railway to the River Yeo, whose confluence with the Dalch lies just upstream. Beyond the footbridge follow the path up to the A377. Traffic is fast and visibility poor. Cross the main road with *extreme care* rejoining the footpath directly opposite. Climb up the field track and turn right into a lane.

Just up the lane stands Bury Barton, an early 14th Century farmhouse once the seat of the Bury family. Tree ring research (*dendrochronology*) has established that the house timbers were felled between 1328 and 1339. Beyond the barton and its imposing courtyard stands a superb 15th Century thatched chapel. Isolated chapels in locations far from churches are not uncommon, but Bury is an enigma. It lies within sight of Lapford church (built 300 years earlier), and it must have stretched even this prosperous farming family's purse to build a chapel for their personal use. The mound on which Bury (from *burh* meaning earthwork) stands also saw use as an Iron Age fort and as the site of a Roman camp dominating the river valley below. This Roman settlement consisted of a small Claudio-Neronian fort, circa 55 A.D., and a military encampment some 4.5 acres in area. It has yet to be

Chapel at Bury Barton

HIKE for HEALTH
SOUTHERN RAILWAY
Go-as-you-please cheap tickets
get you to the country quickest
Ask for details at any S-R Office and buy
Southern Rambles by S-P-B-Mais 6d
DEVON (SR)

excavated. [Further details about Bury may be found in *Old Devon* by W.G Hoskins.]

Continue 0.4 miles beyond Bury to Kelland Cross. Turn left [SP Bow], later passing Kelland Barton, and continue for a further 0.7 miles to Stopgate Cross, a junction with the B3220. (In the 1930s it was not uncommon for farm girls, who'd worked the day shift at the Ambrosia creamery by Lapford station, to cycle here, turn right and pedal six more miles to dances at Winkleigh, where the men were "ever so much more 'ansome," before returning by the light of a battery lantern to Lapford or Morchard Bishop -- all this on fearsomely uncomfortable, gear-less, sit-up-and-beg bicycles!)

Cross the main road with care and continue ahead [SP Zeal Monachorum]. After 0.3 miles, just before a small bridge and milk-churn stand, take a signed bridleway to the left. This leads through Nymphayes Farm (keep dogs leashed) to a road junction. Turn sharp right [SP Down St. Mary] immediately recrossing a somewhat reduced River Yeo, which you last encountered by the railway at Lapford. Yeo (from a Saxon word meaning water) is a common river name in Devon, which is home to at least five. Just to confuse things, *this* Yeo (bound for Barnstaple) is

not connected, other than by name, with the Exeter-bound stream that crosses beneath the platform at Yeoford station.

A one-mile uphill walk brings you to the elevated village of Down St. Mary -- *down*, to add to the confusion, is derived from *dun*, the Saxon word for *hill-top*. St. Mary's Church, on the right, has both Saxon and Norman origins and a fine set of early 16th century pews. Coming out of the churchyard, turn left downhill [SP Morchard Road] and follow the lane down Union Hill for 0.5 miles. At the road junction, turn left and make your way carefully along the A377 for 200 yards to Morchard Road station.

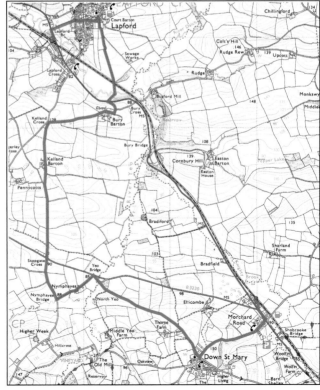

71

LAPFORD

Walk 4. One-way to Eggesford via Nymet Rowland. 5.6 miles. 3.5 hours.
A hill and valley roller-coaster with lovely views and three
(increasingly demanding) uphill sections, this walk (and all those that follow)
explores Henry Williamson's Tarka territory: "the Country of the Two Rivers."
Facilities: Pub (evenings only Mon-Thurs) and stores at Lapford;
Lunch/tearooms and hotel at Eggesford.

As you exit the platform, avoid the main road, and turn immediately left around the back of the station buildings. Do not cross the track, but follow a footpath sandwiched between the railway and the River Yeo past an equipment assembly area. After 200 yards cross the railway on a bridge, and follow the opposite side of the track along a field edge. The path soon veers left and later uphill across two fields and along two further field edges to reach Partridge Farm and the village of Nymet Rowland. Lapford church guards the horizon behind you, and Cawsand (Cosdon) Beacon may be glimpsed to the South.

At the road beyond Partridge Farm continue ahead along the main street to the church at its far end. (As you reach the older properties at the village centre, just beyond a wall mounted post box on the left, note the unsigned right-hand turn by which you'll be leaving the village.) St. Bartholomew's church well repays the few extra steps. It has a fine Norman font of white sandstone and a magnificent 15th Century wooden arcade, one of only two in Devon. Sadly, a mid-Victorian clean-up stripped the churchyard of virtually all its ancient gravestones.

Return to the village road junction and head north. After 0.3 miles, some 200 yards beyond the brow of the hill with Coldridge church clearly visible to the South-west, take a signed

footpath in the left hedge leading steeply downhill towards the River Taw. Nymet Mill, with its ancient barn, nestles in the wood at the end of an enchanting tree-roofed pathway. Out of sight (at least in summer) to your left, the Rivers Taw and Yeo converge. Beyond the

© Carol Coombs

Reception Committee near Nymet Mill.

mill the footpath bends gently right to follow the Yeo upstream. Rejoin the lane and continue ahead, immediately crossing both railway and River Yeo (note the latter's size and pace.)

A few yards beyond, turn left at Nymet Cross T-junction and for 100 yards make your way *very cautiously* along the A377, before escaping into the safety of an unsigned lane leading up through the woods on your right. At a double bend near the hilltop turn left onto a signed footpath, and follow it for 0.6 miles along field edges and past Chenson Farm back to the valley bottom. In May the bluebells are spectacular. Carefully recross the A377, dog-legging 30 yards right along the main road

to enter a bridleway on its far side. After 100 yards, take *extreme care* of children and dogs as you recross the railway at unguarded gates.

Cross the River Taw beyond (comparing the size of the river with the waters of the Yeo, which you left behind at Nymet Cross and which may, or may not, have arrived here ahead of you!) On the far bank turn immediately right along the riverside Tarka Trail, which follows the Taw downstream for 0.3 miles. At a footpath sign, head left and steadily uphill along the field edge. Just before Trenchard Farm (mostly barn conversions), pass a decaying cob barn, but look out for a brand-new cob structure (utilizing cob *bricks*) facing south on the farm's farther side. Beyond, at a lane, turn right, after 0.3 miles reaching Eggesford Fourways crossroads.

Here, at the war memorial cross, turn right through the first gate (*using the foot-dip if provided*) and follow the Tarka Trail along the field edge and (in some years) past organic poultry houses. (Keep dogs under close control.) The path then descends along the field edge to Eggesford Barton's cattle grid, where it turns left along a gravel drive to reach All Saints' church. This not so much a *village* church (there is no village!) as an *estate* church, which stood in the grounds of the original Eggesford House until that house's 19th Century demolition. Restored in 1867, the church interior contains a number of luxuriant memorials to the presiding Chichester and Fellowes families.

Some 300 yards on the left beyond the church is the well stocked Eggesford Garden Centre, whose restaurant offers lunches and teas. The lane ends at a T-junction. Turn right and follow the road for 300 yards, recrossing the river for the final time. Ahead is the station.

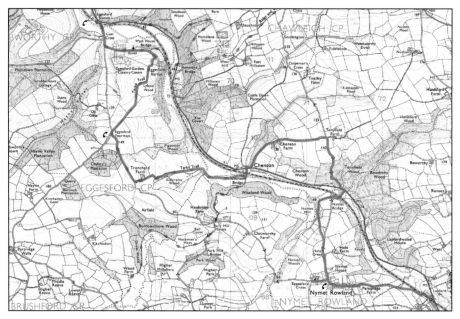

LAPFORD

Walk 5. Home Before Dark. 5.2 miles. 3.25 hours.
A walk through remote countryside takes a nightmarish turn. Fine views. Two steady climbs.
Facilities: Pub (evenings only Mon-Thurs) and stores at Lapford.

At the end of the gated station approach *take particular care* of children and dogs as you cross the A377 and turn left to face the oncoming traffic. Walk over the river bridge (built in 1830 to carry the new turnpike across the Yeo.) After a few yards take the signed footpath to your right, leading up to the village. At the end of the path, continue ahead along the main street, later passing the church. At Orchard Cross, just beyond, keep left [SP Chawleigh] and continue your climb (past two fine bread ovens at Westgate) to the upper end of the village.

Beyond, as you continue your steady climb, look east across the Dalch valley to Morchard Bishop's hilltop church.

In the distant days before the construction of the valley turnpike, the main road

Forches Hill from Handsford Farm

from Exeter to Barnstaple ran, after leaving Crediton, along the ridge through Newbuildings, Morchard Bishop and on to Chawleigh. At Higher *Forches* Cross, where we join this ancient ridgeway, pause for a moment. From our 194 metre (636ft) vantage point, we can see northern Dartmoor's highest landmarks. The massive rounded hill is Cawsand (or Cosdon) Beacon and, further west, stands the jagged outline of Yestor. To the North, the gentler hills of Exmoor are now visible on the horizon.

A major traffic artery in the days of the first Elizabeth, this ridgeway road was then dotted at intervals with a sight guaranteed to capture the attention of passers-by: *forches* or gibbets, from which the decomposing corpses of malefactors were left dangling in the wind to remind the Tudor populace of the penalties of law-breaking. Gibbets were usually sited at intersections where the higher volume of traffic enhanced their cautionary effect. It's hardly surprising that, after nightfall, places such as this were strenuously avoided by God-fearing people.

Bear left [SP Chawleigh]. As its name again implies, the same horrific associations also cast a pall over the next road junction, Lower *Forches* Cross. Again bear left [SP Chawleigh].

Elizabethan travellers following this road to Barnstaple could expect to find plenty more gallows awaiting them. (It's a wonder that today's Barnstaple *Forches* Community Primary School parents aren't fearful for their little ones' safety!) Nor were Exeter-bound travellers along the old ridgeway let off more lightly, having to come face to face with yet another Forches Cross half a mile this side of Crediton. [For further forches encounters, see Portsmouth Arms: Walk 4.]

74

After dropping down to a stream, the old Barnstaple road along which you're walking climbs up to Handsford Farm. At the hill brow shortly beyond, take a signed bridleway on the left. After passing behind the farm and some rusting equipment, the route follows two field edges before entering a gate giving access to a large field. Walk towards Nutson farm's wind turbine. After 200 yards strike out left across the brow of the field, scanning the far hedge (when it appears) for a gated gap reinforced by breeze blocks. This gap marks a footpath junction. Pass through, immediately turning sharp left, and follow the far side of the hedge along a footpath heading directly away from the turbine. This new path reaches a thicket of trees and, beyond, another field providing access to a delightful green way. The way ends at a rather mournful (and marshy!) spot presided over by an abandoned, cob-walled farm. Beyond, take a track leading past a spring and up to the newer (1906) Tonyfield farmhouse. Here turn left onto a lane that descends steeply through bluebell woods to the A377.

Cross this main road with the *greatest care*, and make your way gingerly left along

it for 100 yards to Nymet Cross and the safety of a turning to the right [SP Nymet Rowland]. Cross the River Yeo and the railway in quick succession and continue steeply uphill along the lane for 0.7 miles to the little hilltop village.

At the unsigned T-junction, turn left, following the road to the end of the village where it veers right. At the next (unsigned) intersection, bear left and follow this lane for 0.4 miles to a point, just beyond Lapford's Lower Nymet Farm, where a signed footpath on the left provides a short-cut to the station. *Take extreme care* at the path's far end where you must descend steps and cross the railway track.

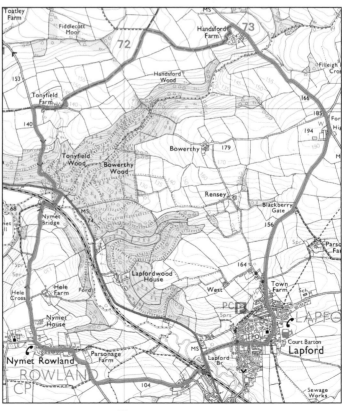

LAPFORD

Walk 6. Aller Bridge & East Leigh. 5.8 miles. 4 hours.
Mostly along country lanes, this is the perfect outing for a fine May day when the hedgerows are at their best. There are lovely views between Leigh Cross and Blackditch.
Facilities: Pub (evenings only Mon-Thurs) and stores at Lapford.

Leave the platform and immediately turn left around the back of the station building, avoiding contact with the main road. After a few yards, *exercise care* as you take a signed footpath leading across the railway line to a flight of steps. Half a century ago several sidings served the Ambrosia Creamery (now Rose Removals) to your left. Beyond the A377 road bridge an isolated, oil-lit "down" platform, reached by an inconvenient wooden staircase from the bridge, once greeted passengers arriving from Waterloo and Exeter.

When the footpath joins a lane at Lower Nymet Farm, with its cobwalled outbuildings and fox weathervane, bear right uphill and continue ahead for 0.4 miles to an unsigned intersection. Keep right and after 40 yards look for a footpath (its sign sometimes concealed) in the left-hand hedge. Take this path along a succession of field edges to reach another lane. Here turn left downhill and follow this lane for the best part of a mile. At about the half-way point the Coldridge Brook briefly keeps you company in the trees to your right.

Just beyond Mizpah Farm (*Mizpah*, meaning watch tower, is an unusual name in Devon) the lane reaches Aller Bridge, a tiny hamlet presided over by Allerbridge Chapel. The name *Aller* (most probably derived from the Low German *eller* and indicating the presence of alder trees) is relatively common -- indeed, there's an Aller Gate just three miles south-west as the crow flies. Turn right over the river bridge, and immediately left

[SP Chilverton]. After 50 yards take a signed footpath on the left which runs parallel to the stream and crosses four fields before arriving at thatched Chilverton farm and Lower Chilverton, a rather startling cobwalled barn conversion. Turn left into a lane, cross the stream and head gently uphill for 0.4 miles to a T-junction at East Leigh, a more substantial farming settlement. Leigh -- from the old English *Leah,* meaning a woodland clearing -- is ubiquitous in Devon, which is home to about 30 (not even counting combinations such as Chaw*leigh* or Chulm*leigh*.) At the junction, dog-leg 50 yards left and continue uphill [SP North Tawton].

At the top of the hill [Leigh Cross] turn left along a lane which follows the ridgeway and offers glorious views (and, should you be interested, the opportunity to spot no fewer than six local church towers!) Looking to your left across the peaceful farming landscape of mid-Devon, it is possible to identify Winkleigh (yet another *leigh*!) perched on its hill away to the West, Coldridge (also with a distinctive hill-top church) directly to the North, and Nymet Rowland, with a less dominant church tower, a little further to the East. On the northern skyline stand the hills of distant Exmoor. After a mile or so, just as the lane drops down to the valley, Lapford (with St Thomas's church half-way up the hillside) becomes visible and St. Mary's Morchard Bishop appears on the north-east skyline ahead. To the East, with good eyes or binoculars, you can make out Down St. Mary's church tower just below the horizon.

The lane descends to the B3220 at Blackditch Cross. (Locals sometimes insert an extra syllable, referring to the intersection as Black-a-Ditch.) Visibility is poor and traffic is fast, so cross the main road with *great care* and, dog-legging a few yards to the right, continue ahead along the lane [SP Lapford]. After very heavy rain this low-lying section occasionally floods but, with luck, you've saved this expedition for a fine spring day, and wet feet are the least of your concerns. Continue for 0.6 miles uphill past a gas installation to reach more level ground graced by Lapford AFC's playing field. Ignore the turning to the left immediately beyond, but keep ahead to Kelland Cross, and here bear left downhill to reach the A377. Turn left past the shop and petrol station, and exercise *extreme care* of children and dogs as you make your way over the railway bridge and back to the station.

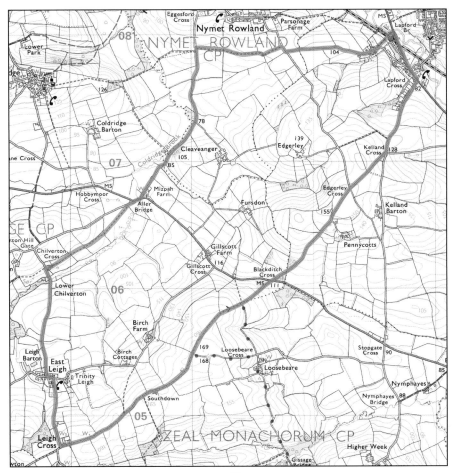

EGGESFORD

All trains stop here and the village would therefore appear to be a place of some importance. Not so. Eggesford has a population of barely 80, its prominent place in the timetable deriving entirely from the fact that the brief section of double track provides a passing opportunity. Since the signal box closed in 1987, tokens ensuring drivers safe access to the single line ahead have been kept in secure containers on each platform.

Walk 1. Bramble ramble to Chawleigh. 6.3 miles. 4 hours.
This varied walk, which follows sections of both the Tarka and the Ridge & Valley trails, is almost entirely along footpaths, and may be muddy. Abundant blackberries.
Facilities: Lunch/tearooms at Eggesford Garden Centre.
Hotel at Eggesford. Pub (closed midday Mon, Tue, Wed.) in Chawleigh.

Leave the station at the level crossing end of the platform and turn right, away from the main road. Cross the River Taw, and shortly beyond ignore the right turn to Wembworthy, taking instead the next turning left [SP Garden Centre]. Pass just below the Centre and make for All Saints' Church 300 yards further on. The church, rebuilt in the 1860s, contains lavish memorials to the Chichester and Fellowes families.

Go through the gate by the church. After 0.2 miles, where the path divides, take the trail [SP Chawleigh] bearing left down to the railway. Accompany the train track over the river before ducking left under the railway. The path veers back along the east bank to a metal corral before crossing the busy A377. On the far side of the road, head up through the forest, ignoring all side turnings. A metal gate at the top leads to a pleasant coomb with a stream. Cross the stream and continue to climb, aiming for a gate near the coomb's upper-right corner. Beyond this gate, skirt West Hill farm and follow the right hedge of

the next field for 0.2 miles to reach a metal gate opening onto a lane. Turn left into the lane. Shortly after it bends left, look in the right-hand hedge for the continuation of the footpath, and follow it over two more fields to Southcott Crossroads. Take the Chawleigh road. Do *not* attempt the slurry-strewn footpath marked on the map, but continue ahead to Shooting Lane Cross. Turn left to Chawleigh.

The name Chawleigh derives from the Saxon word *calveleia* meaning calves' clearing. Since Roman times the village's elevated location -- 165 metres (540 ft) above the Taw and Little Dart valleys -- earned it the responsibility of maintaining a beacon to warn the populace of invasion or other calamity. St. James's Church dates from the 15th Century, and has a fine rood screen.

Sharp-eyed observers may spot signs of the Portsmouth family's life-altering influence, for good or ill, extending up from the turnpike which the family had constructed in the valley.

In 1869, 38 years after this road's completion, a thatch fire destroyed Chawleigh's "London Inn." Though its ridgeway coach trade had already been decimated by the Earl's riverside turnpike, its signboard had remained unaltered. Following the fire, the Portsmouth family rebuilt the pub, renaming it the "Earl of Portsmouth."

Leave the village by the Chulmleigh road heading north-west. At Hollow Tree Cross, the road divides. Take the left (B3042) fork [SP Eggesford Station] for 0.2 miles to Pheasantry Farm. Turn left onto a footpath, following it along the field edge to a dip with a stile on the left. Cross the stile and two footbridges. Head up the right-hand field edge towards a grove of oak trees and, 300 yards beyond, a quiet lane. Turn right and follow this lane to Hilltown Cross. Keep right here

shortly passing Southcott farm. Beyond the farm the route heads clockwise around two sides of a field to reach a muddy dip at the top of a wood. Signage is poor but, in the dip, turn left through a metal gate and follow a wide trail ahead and downhill through the forest to reach the A377.

Eggesford station is just 0.3 miles distant to your right along the main road. *We strongly recommend that you opt for a final mile or so of pleasant walking that does **not** involve contact with A377 traffic:* cross the brook on your right, following its far bank upstream over a stile and through a beautiful coomb. Head up a drovers' way to a metal gate just left of Nethercott's large barn. Pass through the gate and across a further field to reach a road. Turn left and follow this road for 0.6 miles to the station.

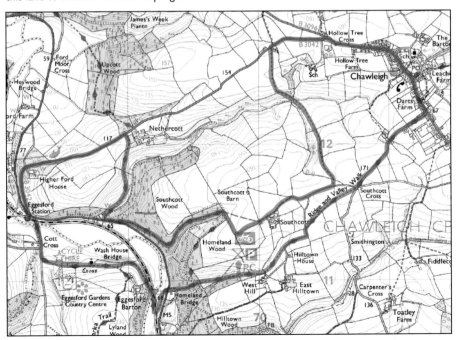

EGGESFORD

Walk 2. Wembworthy. 5.8 miles. 3 hours.
The outbound route briefly follows the Tarka Trail before heading up to
Abbotsham Moor and Wembworthy. May be muddy.
Facilities: Lunch/tearooms at Eggesford Garden Centre.
Hotel at Eggesford. Pub at Lama Cross (closed Sun eve; Mon & Tues).

Leave the station at the level crossing end of the platform. Turn right, away from the main road. Almost immediately cross the River Taw and, shortly beyond, ignore the right-hand turn to Wembworthy, but take instead the next turning left [SP Eggesford Country Garden Centre]. Pass below the Centre and head for All Saints' Church 300 yards further on. The church originally stood in the grounds of Eggesford House, at one time the family home of a branch of the Chichester family, but the old house was demolished in the early 19th Century when the then owner built himself a modern Victorian home further up the hillside. Less than a century later, this new residence had become a ruin, but has since been partially restored. The church, rebuilt in the 1860s, contains several lavish memorials to the Chichester and Fellowes families.

Pass through the gate by the church, noting the old iron gateposts cast by Wright of Sandford. The Tarka Trail follows the gravel drive, but after 0.2 miles, just before the barton, it divides: the Ridge & Valley trail bears left down to the railway, while the Tarka Trail heads right. Follow the Tarka Trail which climbs the next two field edges (in some years passing poultry houses. *Use the foot-dip if provided.* Each house accommodates 500 organically raised free-range birds for the West Country branches of a well-known supermarket). Behind you, across the valley, lies Chulmleigh.

At Eggesford Fourways crossroads there is a well-stocked *agapanthus* nursery. Proceed straight ahead [SP Winkleigh] for 0.8 miles until, shortly after a lane leading off to Hayne Farm on your right, you spot a footpath sign in the right-hand hedge. *[This path – allegedly a short-cut! – is poorly signed, and leads across fields that may be boggy and are ill-supplied with gates. If you're feeling adventurous, keep to the right, aiming for a white cottage at the end of a row of oak trees, where the "path" emerges onto a lane. Turn right.]* An alternative, longer (but possibly faster!) route, is to remain on the road to Partridge Walls crossroads, and here turn right [SP Wembworthy].

This lane continues to Lama Cross, site of the pub and a tractor repair shed. Continue straight on to the little village of Wembworthy, which lies to your right. St. Michael's church, like All Saints' at the start of the walk, was substantially rebuilt in the mid-19th Century. Unless you're visiting the village, continue ahead [SP Staple Green] descending to a stream. After 0.7 miles, at the top of the hill beyond, turn right along a concrete bridleway leading to Higher and Lower Bransgrove. The latter property, glimpsed behind its granite gateposts, is a magnificent Devon longhouse.

Beyond Bransgrove the bridleway continues in the same direction, gradually deteriorating as it follows the field edge down to a fine

stand of ash trees. Once inside Wormsdown Plantation, the path veers left and descends through a coppice of hazel and ash, grown possibly for their walking stick (or charcoal) potential. Follow the increasingly muddy path to the footbridge at the bottom. Pass through the gate beyond and head upward through a field, guided perhaps by the noise of baying hounds, to reach the hunt kennels. Ignore the footpath that leads left at the kennel entrance, and continue up the drive ahead to reach a busy road.

Turn left along the road, and in a few yards follow the more major road [SP Eggesford Station] as it veers right at Heywood Cross and enters Flashdown Plantation. (Care should be taken with children and dogs, for this road carries fast traffic. The intersection is poorly signed, and many a speeding driver has ended up, by default rather than design, making an inadvertent visit to the former Wembworthy Outdoor Education Centre!) Follow the road down through the plantation to reach a T-junction [Cott Cross] at the bottom of the hill.

It's now decision time. Lunches and teas are available to your right; the station lies beyond the river a few hundred yards to your left.

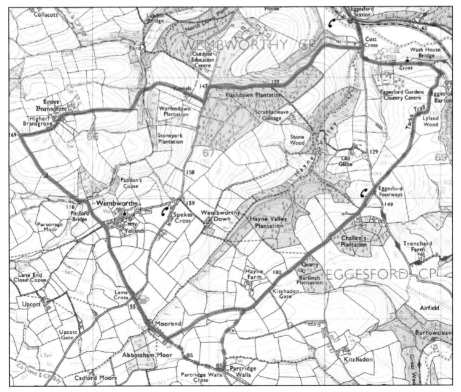

EGGESFORD

Walk 3. Chulmleigh. 5.8 miles. 4.5 hours.
A demanding route, twice crossing the Little Dart valley. Hills are short, but extremely steep!
The final 1.75 mile downhill section comes as welcome relief.
Facilities: Lunch/tearooms at Eggesford Garden Centre. Hotel at Eggesford.
Pubs and shops in Chulmleigh.

Outside the station, cross the busy A377 with great care, and take the quieter B3042 [SP Chawleigh] directly opposite. After 0.8 miles, by Nethercott Farm, turn left along a signed footpath, which begins in a beautiful grove of tall ash trees before leading downhill to a gate and into Upcott Wood. Soon the footpath widens into a track. Where, just before a meadow, this track eventually divides, proceed straight ahead over a stile and ditch, following the footpath across the meadow to a quiet lane.

Turn right, uphill to Chawleigh Week Cross. Proceed straight ahead for 200 yards to Chawleigh Week farm. Here take the *middle* of three tracks, an ancient lane (marked "Unsuitable for Motors" and at one time the established "road" linking Copplestone with Chulmleigh). The way descends, with glimpes of Chulmleigh's church tower, to the Little Dart. (Why *Dart*? Why, indeed? The river rises on Rackenford moor, its only relationship with Dartmoor occurring a mile or so downstream when

Chulmleigh's pump

its waters will merge with those of the Dartmoor-sourced River Taw.) It's worth lingering at the footbridge which crosses the river, a tranquil spot. Note that the upstream faces of the stone piers are V-shaped to slice into the current, while the downstream faces are rounded. On the far side of the bridge brace yourself for a steep pull up Rock Hill to reach the church and the little market town, once famous for its flourishing woollen industry.

The Church of St. Mary Magdalene, dominated by its early 16th Century tower, has a fine rood screen of the same period -- both expensive undertakings made possible by the town's former prosperity. Victorian refurbishment is much in evidence, but fortunately the ancient image of Christ above the inner door of the south porch survived their ministrations. A thatch fire in 1803 destroyed almost 100 Chulmleigh properties, but the subsequent, pre-Victorian rebuilding effort preserved the town's essentially rural atmosphere. Take time to explore.

From the massive village pump (cast by J.D. Young & Son of Barnstaple) head south to the Old Rectory and here keep left (avoiding Chulmleigh Hill) past Copplestones and Davy Park. After 200 yards follow the Old Rectory's rear wall as it curves right into unsigned Egypt Lane (the main road to Exeter until the 1820s). Descend until you reach Egypt Cottage, one of Chulmleigh's oldest and most picturesque homes. Immediately before this cottage take a signed footpath to the left along a field edge to reach a lane. Turn right, dropping down one of Devon's steepest hills (aren't you glad you're not coming *up*?) to a bridge over Huntacott Water followed by a sharp corner at Park Mill Farm. Immediately beyond the bend climb a stile in the right-hand hedge and follow the lower edge of a field to a second stile. Cross this and two parallel leats (which once powered fulling mills downstream) to reach a succession of water meadows. Between the first and the second stands a venerable (but still living) oak trunk. In the third meadow recross the Little Dart on a modern footbridge.

On the far bank the path immediately enters another world: a closely planted conifer plantation, its starkness intensified by the complete absence of any ground vegetation. Beyond in the sunlight, the path soon joins a track. Turn left onto this and shortly bear right to begin

a steady climb through Chawleigh Barton wood, where the detritus of clay pigeon shoots is much in evidence.

At the top of the wood the path forsakes the track and heads just slightly left across two higher meadows. Keep the track in sight below you to the left and walk in a parallel direction to the top of the hill. Here track and path reunite and emerge onto a road. Turn left and walk 50 yards to Hollow Tree Cross. Turn right here and follow the B3042 [SP Eggesford Station] gently downhill for 1.75 miles to the walk's starting point. Refreshments are available at the Eggesford Garden Centre 0.25 miles beyond the level crossing.

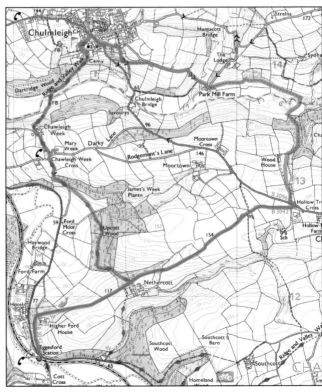

EGGESFORD

Outside the station, cross the busy A377 with great care, and take the quieter B3042 [SP Chawleigh] directly opposite. As you climb, Chulmleigh church tower can be seen peeping over the hill to your left. After 0.7 miles look for a signed footpath in the right-hand hedge just before Nethercott Farm. Turn right and

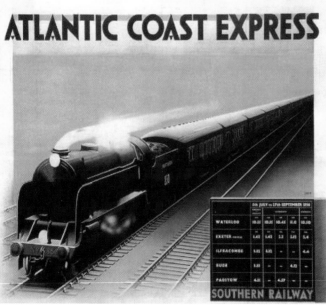

follow this footpath along the field edge to a metal gate. On the far side, an old drovers' way bears to the right down the side of a delightful coomb. As you descend, note how successive generations of sheep have conserved energy by following the contours

along horizontal tracks or *pads* worn into the hillside. At the lower end of the coomb the path runs beside a stream and crosses a stile. It then follows the brook to reach a cluster of buildings, Wash House Cottages. This rather unenviable name recalls the 19th Century practice of Eggesford House, across the River Taw, sending over its dirty laundry.

Turn left along the main road for five yards to cross the stream, and then bear slightly left along a signed bridleway that leads parallel to the main road and gradually uphill. After 0.2 miles, the track veers to the left and the route climbs for a further 0.2 miles, as it ascends the side of a wooded coomb dropping away to your right. A few yards before the top, where a metal gate leads into a field, stay in the forest turning right along a signed [SP Hilltown Wood] track bordering the top of the wood. After 0.2 miles, this track splits into three (an indistinct path to the left, and a choice of two logging tracks leading *ahead* or *slightly right*.) There are no

signs to guide you. Your best bet is to *take the right-hand option for 100 yards down to a well-maintained forest track* running parallel below you, and here to turn *sharp left*. This latter track gently descends for 300 yards to reach an intersection at the edge of the wood. Turn right [SP Eggesford Station] and make your way downhill, ignoring all side turnings, to the Earl of Portmouth's 1831 turnpike (the A377).

Kerslake's iron relief bridge

Cross this busy road taking particular care of children and dogs, and make for the footpath directly opposite. After circling a metal corral, the path veers left across a water meadow to reach the railway, where it passes beneath the track, turns abruptly right and follows a narrow sliver of land between the railway and the River Taw, now immediately to your left. Railway and footpath cross the Taw together, much to the delight of children (and the consternation of dogs!) if a train happens to be passing. Note the old (abandoned) stone bridge 40 yards downstream.

On the farther bank the path separates from the railway and leads uphill, becoming a pleasant treelined track. At the top of the slope, at a fingerpost, the track meets a gravel drive. Bear right along the drive to a gate beside All Saints' Church. There being no

Eggesford village to speak of, this church, rebuilt in the mid-19th Century, functioned primarily to serve the needs of the Chichester and, later, the Fellowes families, owners of Eggesford House. The original house stood close to the church, but in 1828 it was deliberately destroyed by its then owner, the Hon. Newton Wallop, in favour of a more modern structure which he had built on the hillside above. His "improved" residence, however, fell into decay, and has been the subject of extensive renovation by its present owners.

Continue along the drive passing below the Eggesford Garden Centre 300 yards ahead on your left. Beyond, the lane reaches a T-junction. Turn right towards the station. Before crossing the Taw River, note the iron relief bridge constructed in 1868 by Kerslake of Exeter, to reduce flood-water pressure on the original stone structure. (If you lean over the railing you can read the bridge's origin, though perhaps one person in a thousand troubles to do so.) The entry and egress cuts serving Kerslake's bridge have been beautifully paved with stone.

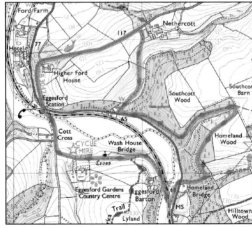

EGGESFORD

Walk 5. The Forestry Commission's First-born. 3.4 miles. 3.5 hours.
More demanding than its short mileage suggests, the walk begins with a prolonged
uphill section. Perfect in late May, when bluebells, campion and wild iris are at their best.
Muddy in spots.
Facilities: Lunch/tearooms at Eggesford Garden Centre. Hotel at Eggesford.

At the level crossing guarding the Exeter end of the platforms turn right, away from the main road, immediately crossing the River Taw on an ancient stone bridge. A few yards further on the lane leads over a flood channel (topped by an iron bridge) to relieve pressure on the old structure. An ancient stone, marked with a "C" just beyond on the left, denotes a boundary, beyond which the County formerly declined responsibility for road maintenance. Ignore the next two side roads -- right to Wembworthy and left to the Eggesford Garden Centre -- but remember the latter's location should you feel peckish on your way back to the station.

Hayne Valley Bridge -- the perfect rest-stop!

Forge straight ahead [SP Brushford] and uphill for 0.6 miles to an intersection [Eggesford Fourways]. The Four Ways, which include the Tarka Trail putting in a momentary appearance on your left, meet by a First World War memorial. Trench warfare, the hallmark of that conflict, (and the coal mining industry's continuous demand for pit-props) consumed vast quantities of wood and, by the war's end, wooded land in the U.K. had dropped to a mere 5% of total land area, the lowest level ever recorded.

To remedy this sorry state of affairs, tree planting began on the Eggesford estate in December 1919. This venture was the very first act of the newly formed Forestry Commission, which during the next 35 years was responsible for the planting of a million acres of woodland throughout the country -- an achievement commemorated here at Eggesford by the Queen's 1956 unveiling of a granite stone in Hilltown Woods just across the A377.

In the last century the Commission was strongly criticised for its perceived lack of environmental awareness but, following the recommendations of Dame Sylvia Crowe in the 1970s, the importance of landscaping began to be recognised on a far wider scale, resulting in plantations which were aesthetically pleasing as well as productive. Woods came to be valued as important wildlife reserves, and conservation

became a special responsibility of Commission staff. In 2011 satellite imagery revealed that 13% of Britain's land area is now wooded -- a vast improvement achieved in the space of a single century.

Bear right at the junction [SP Winkleigh] past a row of estate cottages and continue uphill for a further 0.4 miles. Behind you, across the valley, lies Chulmleigh. The road skirts the edge of Challice's (conifer) Plantation on the left and, a little later, reaches Barlinch (deciduous) Plantation, also on the left. As you arrive at this second stand of trees, be alert for a half-hidden footpath *on the right*, and follow this diagonally across a field to reach a gate guarding the Hayne Valley Plantation. The path follows the edge of this wood before exiting and heading across a field. A metal gate gives access to a muddy path leading down through the trees to a little river and a moss-covered stone bridge -- a delightfully remote resting place.

Climb steeply up the farther bank noting the massive oak -- fallen but not yet dead -- in the field to your right. At the top of the rise, at Wembworthy Down, is a metal gate where the path marked on the OS map has been diverted. Pass through the gate and (avoiding the farm) follow the waymarks up a twisting gravel drive. At a large lambing shed towards the brow, turn right along a newly-minted footpath, entering a field (often with horses). Leave this field and drop back down to the far side of Wembworthy Down to rejoin the original footpath, which follows waymarked field edges before descending gently towards the valley. Enter Stone Wood and cross a tiny side stream. Follow this

stream's farther bank downhill (past, in late May, a glorious display of yellow iris) to a logging track. Turn left along the track for 100 yards, before dropping down to the right to recross the river on another stone bridge.

Follow the muddy logging track beyond as it climbs up through the plantation to the manicured gardens of the Old Glebe. Beyond, the bridleway emerges at a lane. Turn left, downhill. The station lies 0.6 miles ahead, but a brief detour to the right at the bottom of the hill brings you to the Eggesford Country Garden Centre, a good place to celebrate the expedition's completion. Dogs are permitted to keep you company in the tea garden.

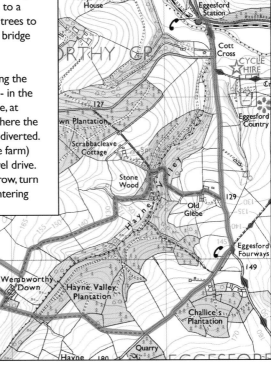

EGGESFORD

Walk 6. Bridge Reeve & Hollocombe Water. 7.6 miles. 5 hours.
After the first mile the walk forsakes the forest and heads off into remote farming country.
Extensive ridgeway views. Plenty of streams for thirsty dogs. Several steep hills. Severe mud
possible along Hollocombe Water.
Facilities: Lunch/Tearooms at Eggesford Garden Centre. Hotel at Eggesford.

At the level crossing turn right, away from the main road. Cross the Taw and after 0.2 miles at Cott Cross turn right [SP Wembworthy]. Follow this road steadily uphill for a mile. Face the oncoming traffic, which sometimes seems ill-prepared for pedestrians, so take particular care of children and dogs. At a sharp bend at the brow [Heywood Cross] turn right onto a quiet lane, almost immediately turning left past the former Outdoor Education Centre. Just beyond, where

Stooks awaiting the thatcher

the lane bears right, take the *second* of two signed paths on the left: a footpath following the edge of North Down Plantation. Where the route first divides, keep left, descending across a forest track to a footbridge. On the far side the path leads up through the trees to meet a track. Turn left (making a mental note of this poorly signed intersection for use on your return) and follow the track up to Labdon farm. Take your bearings. You'll be retracing the steps you've walked thus far, when you return here in three hours' time.

Note the coat of arms on Labdon's south-east gable (indicating that this was once a tenant farm) and the massive beam in the last outbuilding on the right.

Go through the metal gate, immediately turning right (just before an ancient iron plough, now in retirement) past the back of the farm along a signed footpath which soon bears left and divides. Take the *right-hand* option which descends across a field (aim 200 yards left of its bottom-right corner) to Cleave Copse. Cross the stream, and follow the way-markers over two fields to reach a track (with lovely views across the valley to Chulmleigh's church) heading for Gosse's Farm.

Continue ahead to the hamlet of Bridge Reeve where your route merges with a lane from the left. Keep ahead across Hollocombe Water to Bridge Reeve Cross, where the road turns right over Kersham Bridge. Just beyond the fingerpost [SP Dolton], turn left at a footpath sign past Copylake farm's cobwalled barn along a track leading to Bridge Farm. The footpath bypasses the farm and leads along field edges

(note the massive badger setts) above Bridge Wood. Just before a large oak near the bottom of the field, turn left through a wooden gate and follow the path down to a stream, Hollocombe Water, which it then accompanies for the next 1.2 miles. This shady section, with the stream to your left, is delightful (*unless* the farmer has recently driven cattle along the path reducing it in places to a quagmire).

The stream takes its name from Hollocombe, a small village a couple of miles to the South-west. In mediaeval times, Hollocombe was the site of a market and fair, and clearly a place with pretensions -- the northern part of the village even taking on the title of Hollocombe *Town*. These commercial aspirations came to naught as Hollocombe was gradually eclipsed in importance by Winkleigh, but our waterside footpath, the most direct route from the village to the Taw, is very probably ancient.

The path continues along the lower slopes of Horridge Plantation and over a side stream before entering Densham Wood. Beyond a quarry on the far side of the wood the path reaches a lane. Turn left onto this lane immediately crossing the river, and prepare yourself for a stiff climb up the south side of the valley. At the summit at Stable Green, a hamlet with an isolated chapel, turn left. After 0.4 miles, at a sharp left-hand bend, *turn right* at a footpath sign along a farm track, leading first to Collacott's entrance drive, where the track bends left and continues to Labdon. Go through the now familiar metal gate and follow the track by which you arrived, turning right onto "your" footpath at the top of North Down Plantation, and retracing your steps over the stream, up past the former Outdoor Education Centre and back down the hill to Eggesford station.

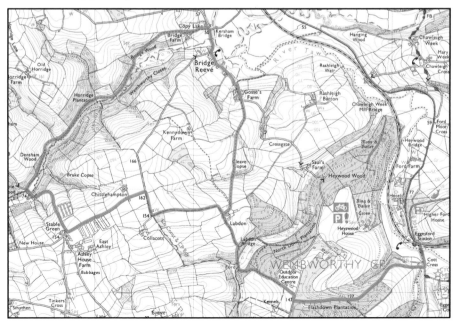

KING'S NYMPTON

For almost a century, until 1951, King's Nympton Station went by the name South Molton Road. The fact that eight miles separated the station from South Molton came as a shock to unwary pedestrians, and doubtless provided good business for the local carrier and nearby hotel. King's Nympton, as we'll now discover, is within easier reach.

Walk 1. King's Nympton Village. 5.9 miles. 3 hours.
Both this walk and King's Nympton: Walk 2 provide an opportunity to spot "green men". Binoculars will come in handy. The route back requires a degree of trust in your author, who will twice be advising you to *disregard* fingerposts pointing to the station!
Facilities: Pub at King's Nympton.

At the end of the station approach, turn left onto the busy A377, taking particular care of children and dogs. After 150 yards, just before the main road crosses the railway, keep right past the former station hotel and along the quieter B3226 for the next 0.2 miles. Shortly after passing Newnham Barton Farm, take a lane that leads off to the right and uphill. Towards the summit the lane turns left and assumes a "deep Devon" look, with grass along its centre, as it follows the hill contours. To your left there are good views across the Mole valley. After 0.2 miles the lane ends at a T-junction by two large oak trees. Turn left here and head steeply downhill.

Where this road meets another lane at Hillhead Cross, turn sharp right [SP King's Nympton] and head along the little valley for 0.7 miles to Catham Bridge. Not far beyond there is a sharp bend. Here the lane crosses the waters of Tongue Lake on crenellated Wooda Bridge and heads uphill past Lower Wooda to reach the village of King's Nympton.

Nympton, like Nymet, is derived from the old Irish word *nemed* meaning grove. The distinguished Devonshire historian, W.G. Hoskins suggested that groves were amongst the earliest Celtic places of worship. With the coming of Christianity, many acquired sacred status as churches were constructed on the ancient sites. Devon is abundantly supplied with Nymptons and Nymets. Readers may recall Nymet Rowland [Lapford: Walks 1. & 4.] earlier in these pages.

King's Nympton -- *which* King is debatable since Kings Harold, William I (the Conqueror), Henry I and Henry III all owned land here -- is a pleasant village with picturesque thatched cottages, some of whose rounded ends indicate the former presence of bread ovens. The church of St. James the Great may well date back to pre-conquest times and, like Burrington across the Taw valley, is home to several "green men". Binoculars will assist in spotting them, but no such help is needed to appreciate the church's superb rood screen. This is probably late 15th Century, a few years earlier than the magnificent one at Lapford. There are numerous box pews, elevated on tiers at the west end, and photographs of the church's

ancient communion plate, on loan to the Victoria & Albert Museum in South Kensington.

Leave the village along the lane by which you entered but, at the bottom of the hill just beyond Wooda Bridge, take the signed public bridleway leading up the hillside to the left. After 0.2 miles the way drops down through trees to cross another stream -- Catham Lake -- by footbridge and ford, before climbing steeply up more open hillside to join a quiet lane. Turn right here and follow the lane for 0.3 miles to a T-junction [Spittle Cross]. Ignoring the fingerpost's suggestion that you head right to reach the station, turn *left* here [SP Cutland] and after 0.3 miles, at Cutland Cross, bear right [SP Elstone] to reach Pyne Meadow crossroads.

The view ahead up the Taw Valley is glorious. Note the old stand for milk churns, partly hidden in the grass bank in front of you. Turn right and continue for a further 0.3 miles to Higher Elstone cross, where the lane bends left, but a public bridleway continues straight ahead. Ignore the fingerpost's exhortation to turn left, and proceed *straight ahead* along the bridleway. Burrington church is clearly visible on the

horizon ahead of you, and there are views back to King's Nympton and the distinctive spire of St. James the Great.

After 0.4 miles the bridleway reaches an intersection at which it is joined by a second way entering from the left. Bear slightly right and downhill, past a refuse tip, for a further 0.4 miles to the road. Turn sharp left to reach the junction with the busy A377, and here bear left and proceed very carefully for a few more yards to reach the safety of the station approach road.

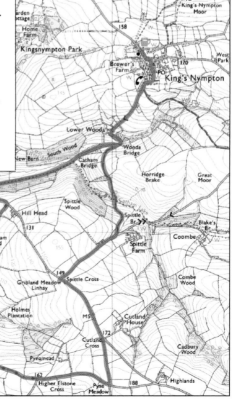

KING'S NYMPTON

Walk 2. Elstone and Burrington. 5.6 miles. 4.5 hours.
Far above the riverside bustle, two tranquil hamlets overlook the Taw.
More "green men" await. Take binoculars!
Facilities: Pub (closed midday Mon, Tue & Thurs.) and village stores in Burrington.

At the end of the station approach, turn left onto the busy A377, taking particular care of children and dogs. Just before the main road crosses the railway, keep right along the quieter B3226 for 200 yards before turning right onto a public bridleway leading uphill. After 0.4 miles, as the ascent starts to slacken beyond an unsightly farm refuse tip, the way divides. Keep right and follow the bridleway up towards the summit, from which there are uninterrupted views across the Taw valley and all the way to the northern hills of distant Dartmoor.

Beyond the hill's brow the bridleway improves in quality before joining a metalled lane at a sharp bend [Elstone Cross]. Proceed ahead to the T-junction beyond Elstone House's wall-mounted letter box and turn right. At the intersection shortly after, continue straight ahead along a very minor lane. This leads to Baker's Elstone Farm, where the metalled surface ends, becoming a public bridleway which descends very steeply down the hillside to reach the A377.

Turn left and follow the A377 with great care for 150 yards. At the intersection by the toll-house, turn right over the railway and the river. Beyond, at Hansford Cross, follow the main road as it bends right -- past Hansford Cottage and Hansford Bridge -- and then veers left. At Mill Moor Cross, remain on the main road. At the next road fork, keep left along a public bridleway, mostly metalled, to reach Golland, a farm largely given over to holiday lets. Turn

Daybreak near Elstone

Image © Derek Harper

right through the farmyard, making for the back of the highest barn conversion where a gate leads to a field-edge bridleway.

At the top of the first large field, a gate opens onto a gravel path, widening into a lane just before it joins the road. Turn left, uphill, onto this road and, beyond another bridleway entering from the left, look for a stile and footpath sign in the right-hand hedge. Turn right, following the footpath diagonally across a field to Hayne Barton farm. Alpacas are raised here; dogs

HIKE for HEALTH
SOUTHERN RAILWAY
Go-as-you-please cheap tickets
get you to the country quickest
Ask for details at any S-R Office and buy
'Southern Rambles' by S-P-B Mais 6d

DEVON (SR)

should be under close control. Where the drive bends right into the farm proper, pass through the metal gate on the left. The footpath divides here. Take the left hand fork which leads diagonally across a field and rejoins the road into Burrington.

There is a splendid old oak in the village square. The modest tower of Holy Trinity Church, just behind it, dates from the 13th Century, though the church was enlarged and a south aisle added two centuries later. It contains a fine wagon roof, and a magnificent decorated rood screen. Holy Trinity is also home to several "green men", ancient decorative motifs. Binoculars should make it easier to spot them.

Leave the village just beyond the pub at Burrington Cross by a road to the right [SP Parish Hall]. Keep right at the first minor junction, continuing on to an intersection where

the road bends left. Keep straight ahead along Twitchen Lane. Shortly after the lane bends right, take a signed footpath in the left-hand hedge by two large metal gates. The footpath follows the field edge (where the foxgloves in June are quite exceptional), and descends down a second field to a gully, where the path now diverges from the OS map.

Once across the gully, head for the gate at the far top corner of a third field. Pass through and follow the upper hedge beyond until a footpath sign by a gate points left along a field edge to a lane. Turn right along the lane past Catham Farm's entrance drive (sounds of the farm's vibrant agricultural activity contrast pleasantly with the forlorn atmosphere of Golland's holiday rentals) and descend for 0.6 miles to the A377. Turn right, facing the oncoming traffic and *take great care* as you follow the busy road for 0.3 miles across the river to the station.

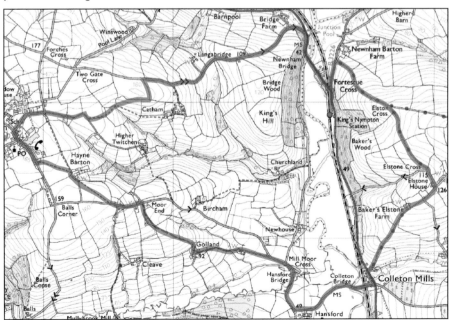

KING'S NYMPTON

Walk 3. One-way to Eggesford Station via Chulmleigh.
5.7 miles. 3 hours.
A walk along the high ridge lying east of the River Taw. Chulmleigh parish is
home to the largest population of wild otters in England.
Facilities: Pubs and shops in Chulmleigh. Lunch/tearooms & Hotel at Eggesford.

From the platform follow the station approach, turning left onto the busy A377. Face the oncoming traffic taking special care of children and dogs. At Fortescue Cross by the former railway hotel, bear right along the quieter B3226. After 200 yards or so, turn right up an unsigned public bridleway. After the ascent becomes less steep, the ridgeway forks.

Keep left for a further 0.4 miles to reach a bend in a lane [Higher Elstone Cross]. Proceed straight ahead along the lane for 0.3 miles, enjoying the view of distant Dartmoor, to Pyne Meadow Cross. Note the old milk-churn stand, partially hidden in the grassy bank on the right, and turn right [SP Chulmleigh]. The road proceeds gently downhill before dropping steeply to cross Ford Brook at Trunk Bridge, then follows the edge of Longmoor Wood as it climbs once more to higher ground. After 1.2 miles, at Bond's Cross, join a more major road and continue ahead at Four Crossways

past the college into Chulmleigh. With the walk more than half completed, the little market town provides an opportunity to restore the tissues. It is also home to a welcome number of independent retailers.

Chulmleigh began its days as a Saxon settlement, its name probably deriving from *Ceolmund's Leigh*, a reference to the 9th Century Saxon who recognised the hilltop's worth both as a defensive site and as a source of fresh meat.

In the Middle Ages Chulmleigh, like Crediton, established itself as a wool town. The impressive church of St. Mary Magdalene, with its painted bosses and carved rood screen, testifies to the prosperity which the woollen industry bestowed. An old rhyme put it succinctly: "I praise the Lord and ever shall, for that the sheepe hath paid for all!"

The town's annual fair has 13th Century origins and, as late as 1850, William White

OLD COUNTRY TOWNS
IN SOUTHERN ENGLAND
via Southampton Docks or the short sea routes of the
SOUTHERN RAILWAY

HIKE for HEALTH
SOUTHERN RAILWAY
Go-as-you-please cheap tickets
get you to the country quickest

Ask for details at any S-R Office and buy
"Southern Rambles" by S-P-B-Mais 6d

DEVON (SR)

noted the existence of a weekly corn & cattle market, a monthly livestock market and "two large fairs." Alas, Chulmleigh's days were already numbered, as the 1831 turnpike road (now the A377) and, a quarter-century later, the railway diverted trade and transport away from the ridge and down to the Taw valley below. The Market House (now the "1894" Town Hall) was erected in 1849 at a cost of £300 in a last-ditch effort to boost the town's declining fortunes, but never saw the activity for which it was originally intended.

From the south gate of St. Mary's church, head a few yards right past Glebe Cottage to the top of Rock Hill, where an ancient track once led all the way to Copplestone. This path descends steeply along the edge of Dartridge Wood to cross the Little Dart River on a footbridge. It's well worth pausing here. Continue along the ancient lane as it climbs the south side of the valley to arrive at Chawleigh Week farm. Here you are joined by a track entering from the right. The farm gates are no more, but their massive hinges remain. Continue ahead to a staggered crossroads [Chawleigh Week Cross]. The local names are delightful: James's Week Lane leads to your right; Darky Lane to the left.

Your route, however, lies straight ahead following the lane down a steep descent. Near the bottom take the footpath [SP Eggesford Forest] leading off to the left across a field to a stile. Follow the track ahead uphill through Upcott Wood. Later the track dwindles to a path, passing through a gate and a grove of stately ash trees to emerge at

a road opposite Nethercott Farm. Turn right and follow this road for 0.8 miles down to Eggesford station.

By now some sort of refreshment is probably in order. The tearooms lie five minutes' walk away, over the level crossing and the river and then first on the left.

KING'S NYMPTON

Walk 4. Mullybrook and Colleton Mills. 5.1 miles. 3.5 hours.
A varied walk along both sides of the Taw valley. Muddy and poorly signed in places.
No refreshments, so take a picnic!
Facilities: None.

At the end of the station approach, turn left and with *great care* make your way along the A377 [SP Barnstaple] facing the oncoming traffic. Follow the main road over the railway for 0.2 miles. Immediately after crossing the River Taw at Newnham Bridge, turn left [Riverside Cross] along an unsigned lane that accompanies the river upstream. After 0.5 miles, just beyond a little brook, be alert for a track (with a footpath sign set well back) leading right. Follow this path past Churchland, where the route bears uphill along a green lane and enters a succession of fields. Signage is poor, but follow the footpath along field edges and over stiles aiming just to the right of Bircham Farm, the buildings on the hill above you. Here the path emerges at a road.

Turn right, uphill, and follow this road for 0.4 miles, ignoring signed paths leading first to the right and then to the left. At Cleave Down, turn left along a bridleway leading downhill. The bridleway continues all the way down to Mullybrook, the stream at the valley bottom. Mullybrook Mill and its ancient leat lie on the far side of the bridge. Just beyond the mill turn left along a signed bridlepath. This passes Fox Meadow, a delightful

cottage, and then follows the lower contours of the valley before entering Hansford Plantation. Once in the trees the path bears right along a logging track through the wood until it reaches a quiet lane. Turn left and follow this lane for 0.3 miles to a T-junction.

Turn right here and follow the road over the River Taw and the railway line to the A377 crossroads, presided over by a former tollhouse (easily identifiable by the protruding doorway facing the Exeter to Barnstaple turnpike). This custom-made road, constructed between 1828 and 1831 by a consortium which included the Hon. Newton Fellowes of Eggesford, revolutionised local transportation and put paid to the dreams of many a ridgetop village. An active investor, Fellowes was MP for North Devon (1832-1837) and in 1853 became Earl of Portsmouth.

Installation of McAdam road surface, circa 1830.   Carl Rakeman

The Exeter Turnpike Trust (founded 1753) was unusual in that it managed 147 miles of road, far more than the typical trust purview of about 20 miles. The quality of early turnpikes varied widely, but Exeter had the good sense to engage the famous engineer John Loudon McAdam (1756-1836) as its consultant surveyor, and it was he who oversaw the route and construction of the Exeter to Barnstaple road. McAdam had firm opinions about road-bed composition. He insisted on a careful selection of broken stone ("no piece to weigh more than six ounces") laid in a tight symmetrical pattern, and covered with fine chippings to produce a smooth running surface -- a process that came to be known as "McAdamising". (Results were dramatic: by 1843 the Exeter to London coach could complete in just 17 hours the 170 mile journey that had once taken more than a week -- an achievement, in its turn, to be eclipsed by the performance of the railway.)

At the Colleton Mills tollhouse, turn left [SP Barnstaple] along the grass verge and make your way for 120 yards to Colleton Mill Farm. Turn right, carefully crossing the A377 to enter a lane marked "Unsuitable for Motors." The ascent is steep. At the summit the track, now metalled, is joined by a lane from the right. Keep ahead for 200 yards to an unsigned intersection by a wall-mounted letter box, and here turn left past Elstone House. At Elstone Cross, where the road bends left, keep ahead along an unsigned track between hedges. This ridgeway offers lovely views, later being joined from the right by a second track and descending to the Mole valley, where it ends at a road. Turn sharp left and follow this road to its intersection with the A377. Bear left along the main road and carefully make your way to the station entrance.

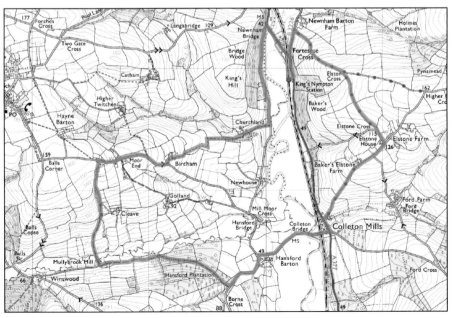

97

PORTSMOUTH ARMS

One wonders how many bewildered travellers, confused by the name, have inadvertently ended up in this isolated hamlet. Lucky them, for the location is idyllic.

The River Taw has now assumed impressive proportions, yet is dwarfed by the surrounding hills. The station's name, shared by the local pub, reflects the activities of a 19th Century Earl of Portsmouth. The Earl was involved in the development of the Barnstaple to Exeter turnpike along the Taw, Yeo and Creedy valleys, an enterprise which put paid to the fortunes of many a ridge-top village. Maid of Kent, a first-class Pullman coach, awaits refurbishment.

Walk 1. One way to Umberleigh via Chittlehamholt.
6.6 miles. 4 hours.
This walk, mostly along tranquil lanes, may be tackled after wet weather.
Facilities: Pubs at Portsmouth Arms, Chittlehamholt and Umberleigh.

Leave the station, and turn right along the busy A377 taking particular care of children and dogs. Global warming notwithstanding, motorists driving from Barnstaple to Exeter are encouraged by the signage to add an extra 16 miles to their journey and travel via Tiverton Parkway. Despite these exhortations, the Earl of Portsmouth's turnpike venture, now the A377, still carries heavy traffic.

Directly opposite the Portsmouth Arms pub, cross the road with care and follow an unsigned lane uphill to a T-junction. Turn right to reach the little hamlet of Kingford, a name that indicated a safe river crossing in the days before bridges. *Which* king is debatable, but in the early 10th Century Athelstan, the grandson of cake-burning Alfred and the first king of "all England," maintained a palace at Umberleigh, four miles downstream.

Recross the A377 with care and proceed directly ahead [SP Chittlehamholt] over the River Taw on a bridge built only in 1909 -- one third of its cost being met by

public subscription. Beyond the railway bridge the road rises steeply past Presbury and continues for a further 1.4 miles to a T-junction [Cholloway's Cross]. Turn right here, keeping an eye out for a kissing gate in the left-hand hedge. From this gate a footpath leads alongside a golf course and across several fields to the hamlet of Chittlehamholt.

At the end of the footpath, with the pub a stone's throw to your right, turn left into the main street and at the first intersection left again to follow a road [SP Portsmouth Arms] leading out of the little community. After 0.3 miles at Drake's Cross a minor lane leads off to the right [SP Spycott]. Take this lane and follow it for 0.5 miles. Just before Spycott, where the lane veers left, look for a bridleway sign on the right. High Bickington and Atherington church towers are both visible across the valley. Follow the bridleway downhill to a wood, where the route divides. Turn left and continue along the bridleway for roughly the same distance before turning right and descending to an idyllic ford and

footbridge. Once across the stream, bear left at the top of the slope to join a metalled lane that follows the lower contours of the valley to reach Park Farm, 0.3 miles distant.

Beyond Park Farm, join a road and follow it in the same direction along the valley bottom. For the next 1.9 miles the railway and the River Taw keep you company on your left until, just beyond Park Gate, the lane crosses the railway and continues for a short distance to Umberleigh. Until a comparatively recent post office reorganization, Umberleigh was the unlikely location of a sorting station for the "largest postal catchment area in England," requiring the services of an eleven member staff. The railway station lies a few yards to your right along the B3227.

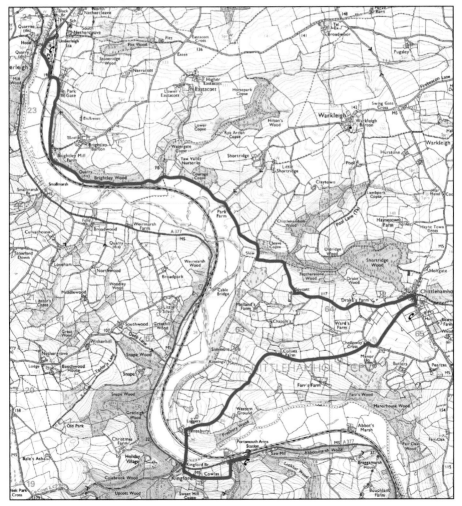

99

PORTSMOUTH ARMS

Walk 2. High Bickington. 7.3 miles. 5 hours.
A demanding hike along lanes, footpaths and bridleways which can be
muddy after rain. The walk begins with a steady uphill slog, rewarded
by lovely views across the Taw valley.
Facilities: Pubs at Portsmouth Arms and High Bickington.

On leaving the station, turn right along the busy A377 taking particular care of children and dogs. Directly opposite the Portsmouth Arms pub and its fine old barn, cross the road with caution and follow an unsigned lane steeply uphill to a T-junction. Turn left here [SP Northcote] and continue uphill with the woods of Northcote Manor on your left. After 0.9 miles, the lane ends at a T-junction [Northcote Cross]. Turn right [SP Torrington] and follow this more major road for 0.4 miles to a sharp bend to the right [Five Oaks Cross]. Continue along the main road past two minor lanes leading to Upcott and Southcott, to reach Dole Park Cross East, where the road divides. Take the right-hand fork past an ancient milestone. After 0.15 miles at an unsigned intersection just beyond Briony, turn right (downhill at last!) to reach a T-junction.

Turn right past Week farm noting the old stone roller and railway wagon. Beyond the farm by a barn on the left, a metal gate leads to an unsigned right of way between high banks. Go through the gate and follow the soft-bottomed track as it curves left towards the western edge of Upcott Wood. The track ends at a road running through a wooded coomb. Turn left, uphill, along the road but, as soon as the wood on your right ends, take the narrow lane on that side of the road, and follow it past Bale's Ash to a T-junction. Turn right here, keeping alert for a footpath sign at the end of the first field to your left. From here you can just see the tower of High Bickington church. Turn left onto the footpath which leads across four

fields to reach a road. Turn left and make your way to the village.

The ridgeway village of High Bickington, set like its neighbours Burrington and Atherington far above the Taw valley, offers fine views extending all the way to Exmoor. All three villages share that rather wistful air of having being left high and dry, their lofty isolation having cut them off from the transportation changes taking place along the river during the last 250 years. High Bickington claims 7th Century Saxon origins, and a thousand years later had developed into a community of some local importance. Until the 18th Century the village held both a spring and an autumn fair in addition to a weekly market.

The unremarkable housing along the B3217 is deceptive. The older part of the village lies a few yards west and offers cobbled pavements, a second pub, and a still functioning (in 2012) post-office with a metal sign describing its

mid-20th Century services. St. Mary's Church has lost its shady avenue, but still boasts an unusual decorated cobble path. Inside, the

misaligned wagon roof and carved bench-ends, dating from the 14th to the 19th Century, are a delight.

Leave the village along the lane by which you entered. Ignore "your" footpath but continue ahead past a memorial bench to Beechwood House lodge. Turn sharp right ignoring the drive and follow the signed avenue, which reverts to a footpath skirting Beechwood House and leading across two fields and through a wood guarded by stiles to a further field, where it drops steeply down to a cottage. Turn right here and follow Taylor's Lane, as it's known, to a road junction. "Your" former footpath is just to the right, but continue ahead,

and take the first turning on your left, passing Bale's Ash once more, to reach the road. Turn left and head steeply downhill. Colebrook Wood lies to your left, Upcott Wood to the right. At the bottom of the hill, the road reaches the busy A377 at a T-junction. Turn right and immediately right again up an unsigned lane through the hamlet of Kingford. A gentle 0.25 mile ascent along the lower contours of the hillside brings you to a lane leading off to the left, marked by a fingerpost high in the hedge. Turn left and descend to the Portsmouth Arms pub and the A377. The station lies a few yards to your right. Take particular care of children and dogs as you make your way back.

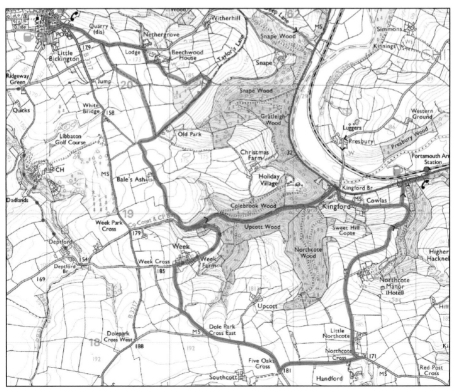

PORTSMOUTH ARMS

Walk 3. Cotts, Cotes and Weeks. 4.75 miles. 3.25 hours.
An invigorating hike to remote ridgeway farms beginning with a
160 metre (525 ft) climb. Good views.
Facilities: Pub at Portsmouth Arms.

Leave the station and turn right facing the oncoming traffic as you carefully make your way along the busy A377. Opposite the Portsmouth Arms pub cross the road and take an unsigned lane uphill to a T-junction, presided over by a (sometimes overgrown) fingerpost high in the left hedge. Turn right and descend gently to the cluster of houses that comprise Kingford.

Turn left along the A377 for 15 yards before ducking left [SP Burrington] along a road which ascends between two deciduous woods: Colebrook Wood (right) and Northcote Wood (left). A stream provides pleasant company and the opportunity for accompanying dogs to slake their thirst. After 0.7 miles of steady climbing (some 200 yards beyond a holiday home development on the right), be alert for an unsigned track leading left, over a stone faced, wooden fenced bridge across the stream and into the trees. Take this public right of way which climbs to the top of Upcott Wood. *Upcott*, meaning "higher cottage," is a common Devon name and

there are more than 40 Upcotts (or Uppacotts) in the county. *Endicott*, "far-flung or end cottage," is also ubiquitous (both as a place name and surname), and there are numerous other variants on the same theme, e.g. *Southcott*, *Northcott*, *Westacott*, *Eastacott* and *Nethercott*.

The path emerges from the trees and follows an ancient way up the hill with increasingly fine views back across the Taw valley. In spring and early summer the hedges are ablaze with wildflowers, though the going can be soggy. The way curves gently to the right as it climbs to reach a gate opening onto Week Farm. *Week* typically denotes just the sort of small, often isolated, farming community you encounter here, and the name is also widespread, with some two dozen *Weeks* or *Weekes* scattered throughout Devon. Continue ahead past the farm, noting the old railway wagon pressed into agricultural service and the ancient stone roller (which must have required the motive power of exceptionally strong

Upcott Wood

© John Ward, Bideford www.megapiks.co.uk

horses). Just beyond Higher Week, take the first turning to the left along an unsigned lane leading up to a road.

Turn left and follow this road to Dole Park Cross East (noting the fine milestone on the right just before the intersection). Bear left, with Warkleigh church visible across the valley to your left. Ignore side-turnings to *South*cott and *Up*cott to reach Five Oaks Cross, where the main road bends sharply left. Here a signed footpath leads right. Follow this path through two gates in quick succession, then right along the upper edge of the first large field (with views to Dartmoor's Cawsand Beacon and Yestor). On the field's far side, go through the gateway nearest Southcott, passing left of the farmhouse and gently downhill across fields and over a double stile to reach a gate at the valley bottom. Beyond, a stream flows down from Southcott (or Great Halfsbury) Moor. Once over the water, veer left and diagonally uphill across the field on the farther side, before turning right and following two field edges to emerge onto a quintessential Devon lane. (Its mossy surface and the ancient biplanes taking off from nearby Eaglescott Airfield almost persuade you that you're back in the 1930s.) Turn left along the lane, recrossing the stream and then gaining ground as you ascend to Halfsbury Cross intersection.

Here dog-leg slightly to the left across the main road and follow

the signed footpath along a concrete track to a green metal barn. Bear left, following the footpath across two fields (populated, in 2009, by free-range chickens) with views of Burrington church. At Handford Farm, keep dogs under control as you navigate your way just right of the house, rejoining the main road at the end of the front drive, beyond a well-house and former watercress pond. Turn right for 100 yards, and at Northcote Cross, turn left [SP Portsmouth Arms]. After a while, you're rewarded with superb views (marred only by the aforementioned holiday home development) and a steep, well-deserved descent. Pass Little Northcote, and later on your right the wooded boundary of Northcote Manor (now an hotel), to reach an intersection. Turn right and continue downhill to the Portsmouth Arms pub. Turn right facing the oncoming A377 traffic and exercise *great care* as you make your way back to the station entrance.

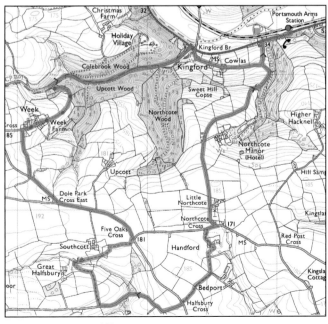

PORTSMOUTH ARMS

**Walk 4. One-way to King's Nympton Station via Burrington.
4.8 miles. 2.75 hours.**
A steady climb of 143 metres (470 ft) is repaid by superb views ...
... and a dreadful warning.
Facilities: Pub at Portsmouth Arms.
Village stores and pub (closed midday Mon, Tue & Thurs.) at Burrington.

Turn left along the busy A377 facing the oncoming traffic and taking particular care of children and dogs. After 300 yards, just beyond a stream, turn right into the safety of a lane [SP Burrington] and follow the stream uphill. At an intersection 0.4 miles later, turn right [SP Burrington] and continue mostly uphill for 1.3 miles passing Bouchland, Ley and Hill Farms to Forches Cross and its elevated brazier beacon.

The views are spectacular and there's a bench that makes a good resting place ... provided, that is, you're not easily unnerved. For *forches* means gallows, and this peaceful spot was at one time the site of a prominent gibbet. Here the miscreant (whose alleged offence might be no more than the theft of a sheep to feed a starving family) would be dragged and summarily hanged, his body left to swing in the breeze as a grisly warning to passers by. In 16th Century Devon this practice was widespread. John Hooker, in his 1584 *Description of the Citie of Excester* [Exeter] shortly before the enactment of the Elizabethan Poor Law, records that the authorites "commanded Forches and Gallows to be set up in Sundry places" to discourage crime. Crossroads located at points of 16th Century traffic density provided maximum cautionary value, and remain the best places to spot a "forches cross." (Crediton and Newton Abbot both have a Forches Cross, while Lapford [see Lapford: Walk 5.] went one better with a "Higher" and a "Lower" Forches Cross a mile north of the church.)

A word before we leave. It was not normally the custom to accord malefactors, unless of rank, a churchyard burial, and the state of the victim's body after a few weeks out in Devon rain or sunshine did not encourage transportation by those charged with cutting it down. Interment as close to the gibbet as possible was much the most convenient, and there is probably good reason why the grass here grows so lushly.

From the crossroads continue straight ahead [SP Burrington] for 0.2 miles. At the Twitchen Lane fingerpost where a lane enters from the left, turn sharp right (remember this corner as you'll be leaving the village this way) and continue past the parish hall. The ancient oak guarding the entrance to Holy Trinity Church was in all probability a full-grown tree at the time of the first Elizabeth. The church contains a Norman font, and traces of 13th Century masonry have been identified at the base of the tower and along the north wall of the nave. The building was enlarged in the 15th Century with the addition of a south aisle, south porch and granite perpendicular windows. Its rood screen and wagon roof are very fine, no doubt reasons for its Grade 1 architectural listing. "Green men" -- ancient fertility motifs usually featuring the image of a face with foliage coming from the eyes, nose or mouth -- are also in evidence, and best examined through binoculars.

Leave the village as you entered. At the corner where "your" entry road turns

104

left, continue as directed by the fingerpost *straight ahead* along Twitchen Lane following it round a right-hand bend to its destination at Higher Twitchen Farm. Here turn right over a signed stile leading steeply downhill to a metal gate and stream. Head up the far bank to a gate and along the field edge beyond to reach a lane. Turn left along this lane for 0.2 miles to a signed footpath leading left to Bircham Farm. At the farm the footpath turns right along the left-hand hedge of a large field. Signage is poor. About 200 yards below Bircham take the first gate in the hedge, pausing to identify a stile at the lower end of the next field about 100 yards from its bottom corner. Head for this

stile, which leads down along a field and track to the stream that you crossed earlier at Twitchen. Churchland farm lies at the bottom of the steep little valley. Follow its entrance drive to reach a T-junction with a lane. Turn left and follow this lane along the base of King's Hill. Soon the River Taw joins you. Beyond it stands your destination: King's Nympton station. The peaceful lane offers a welcome refuge from the bustling traffic along the A377. All good things, alas, must end. At Newnham Bridge, where the lane joins the main road, turn sharp right over the river and make your way with *great care* along the A377 for 0.2 miles to reach the safety of the station's approach road.

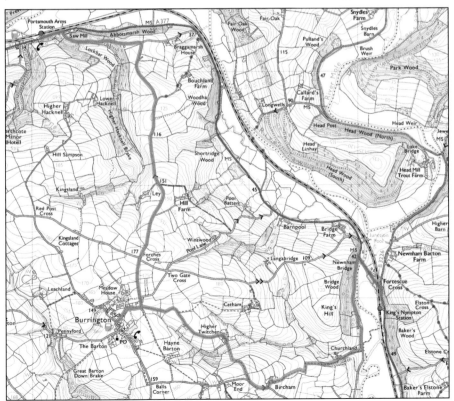

UMBERLEIGH

Nestled in a glorious wooded valley, Umberleigh remains a peaceful wayside halt. The community's original function was as a crossing point, most recently by the graceful three-arched bridge (rebuilt 1915), over the River Taw on the road between South Molton and Great Torrington. The river offers fish -- salmon, sea and brown trout -- in abundance, a fact not lost perhaps on Athelstan, the first king of "All England," who built a palace and chapel here in the early 10th Century.

Walk 1. Umberleigh to Chapelton. One-way. 4.1 miles. 3 hours.
A walk to the hilltop village of Atherington and along the hills bordering the west bank of the River Taw. Those in search of a more demanding day out may wish to combine this walk with Chapelton: Walk 1. -- a 7.6 mile round-trip.
Facilities: Pub at Umberleigh.

(Chapelton)

Umberleigh provides further evidence of the line as it once was. Note, for example, the number of arches on the road bridge at the platform's north end, which easily spanned the double track that was removed in 1971.

Leave the station and head across the bridge carrying the B3227 over the river. Note Murch Brothers' former tractor works (now an antiques emporium) on the right.
At the T-junction with the A377 head carefully across the main road to take a bridleway leading steeply uphill to the right of the pub. A disused quarry lies immediately to your right. At a slanted T-junction, where the bridleway rejoins the B3227, bear left uphill for 0.4 miles keeping children and dogs under close control.

In a dip shortly beyond the first [Fisherton Cross] intersection watch for a footpath sign in the left-hand hedge opposite Riverlake Cottage. Leave the road here and make your way alongside a stream at the bottom of a muddy field in the direction of a corrugated iron barn by a stile. Beyond the stile lies a pretty bluebell wood. The path now bears right to follow field edges leading up to a minor crossroads. Turn right here and enter the attractive hilltop village of Atherington, whose church tower forms a distinctive landmark for miles around. Note the railway sleepers pressed into service for a milk-churn stand on the green across from the church.

The 15th Century Church of St. Mary is well worth a visit, not least for the fact that it contains the only surviving rood-loft remaining in the county. This dates from the first part of the 16th Century. Now confined to the north aisle, it would once have reached right across the chancel. One window, also in the north aisle, retains its mediaeval glass.

From the crossroads in the centre of Atherington, just to the left of the church,

take a road [SP Fishleigh Barton] leading north out of the village. Almost immediately this road divides and at the fork, where the main road begins to descend, bear left along a very minor unsigned lane. After 0.4 miles this lane bends sharply left. One field further along, at a T-junction, turn right along a lane leading gradually downhill. After 0.3 miles, take a signed footpath in the left-hand hedge, and follow the field edge downhill to enter a wood. The pleasant path continues -- with much evidence of rabbits in the bank to your left -- to reach a small stream and a footbridge. Cross the stream, bear right over the stile and then steeply up the left-hand flank of the coomb ahead. The top of this coomb is under attack by Japanese knotweed. Pass through Furzedown farm, and follow a concrete drive past the newly built bungalow and a further field to emerge onto a quiet lane.

Turn right into this lane, and continue gently downhill. At Langley Cross proceed straight on. Chapelton station lies only a mile ahead, just across the busy A377.

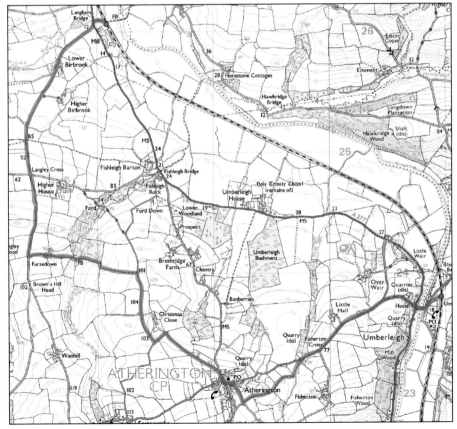

UMBERLEIGH

Leave the station and take the B3227 over the railway towards South Molton. After a few yards, turn right at a footpath sign, passing below the primary school. Follow the drive (a public right of way) to South Nethercleave where it turns left and becomes a grassy footpath leading to a metal gate. North Nethercleave Farm (out of sight to your left) was formerly the South-west's only snail farm, supplying a number of Devon restaurants.

Go through the gate and follow the next field-edge clockwise beside a stream and uphill to Pitt Wood, beyond which the route divides. Keep right and uphill through a plantation to reach a gate and stile. Pitt farm is on your left. Head up the farm lane to a road, where a five minute diversion down the road *to your right*, takes you to a wayside cross, offering superb views. Your route from Pitt farm lane, however, lies a few yards along the road *to the left*, away from the cross, to Eastacott Crossroads. Here, turn right and follow the Warkleigh road for 0.2 miles to a gate (and partly hidden footpath sign) in the left-hand hedge.

Follow this footpath for 0.8 miles. Aim for the oak tree and gate on the far side of the first field, then keep left of the cob barn. Cross the stile beyond and continue with the field edge on your left. *Be alert for a gate* in the hedge, where you must change sides and continue with the hedge on your right. The path follows more field edges to reach a lane. Turn left over

a stream and past cottages to Homedown Crossroads. Cross the main road, and later, after the lane bends left, look for a footpath (sign almost hidden in the right-hand hedge) which leads along a passage, over a stream and up to Chittlehampton.

Accounts of Chittlehampton's most famous daughter, Urith (or Hieritha), vary. It was in the 6th (or possibly the 8th) Century that a group of heathen Saxons (female, and perhaps urged on by the victim's pagan stepmother) hacked to death a young Christian girl named Urith. A holy spring (now capped by the well near Rose Cottage at village's east end) bubbled up at the site. The original church was built over Urith's burial place. Her Saint's Day is 8th July, and pilgrimages to her grave were common until the mid-16th Century establishment of the Church of England, when St. Urith's was largely rebuilt. The tower, worthy of a cathedral, is among the finest in the county.

Make for the village square's top right corner, where a footpath leads across three fields to a lane. Cross the lane and stile opposite and head down the field edge to a footbridge. Climb the hill beneath the pylons, to reach East Stowford, Urith's birthplace. Where the path meets a lane, turn left and continue for 0.4 miles. At the next junction bear right [SP Cobbaton]. After 0.3 miles bear right again [SP Cobbaton] and then left at Puddlepool Cross [SP Lower Cobbaton]. After 0.3 miles, at

Lower Cobbaton Cross, turn left immediately passing the Cobbaton Combat Collection, an amazing assortment of wartime paraphernalia assembled by Preston Isaac, who admits that the collecting bug that bit him as a schoolboy has got rather out of hand! Should you wish to add additional weight to your backpack (there's only about 1.75 miles left to go!) or to complete your walk by some more distinctive method of transportation, many items are for sale.

Follow the lane 0.4 miles beyond the museum. Where it bears left, take a footpath (doubly signed!) in the right-hand hedge, aiming for the gorse clump 200 yards left of the farm opposite. Beyond the gorse, a footbridge leads

to an old orchard and Hawkridge Barton, a magnificent thatched building with a fine, as yet unconverted, barn. Just beyond the barton, turn left to follow a footpath steeply up the field edge. From the summit [Hawkridge Cross] you are rewarded with glorious views. Continue ahead [SP Umberleigh] and downhill.

At the bottom of the hill, just before the lane bends left, take a signed footpath to the right and follow this path down to the River Taw, where the footpath turns left. Follow the path upstream to Umberleigh. The pub is across the river bridge. The station lies to your left, just a few yards up the B3227 in the direction of South Molton.

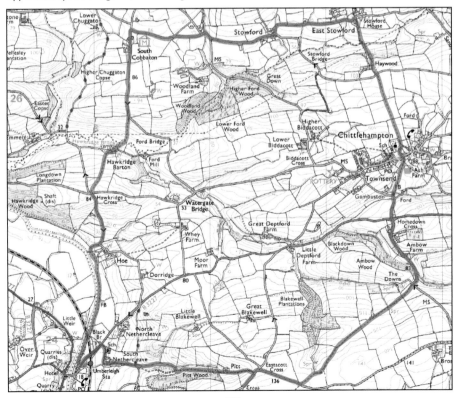

UMBERLEIGH

Walk 3. Moats and Crosses. 3 miles. 2 hours.
A short outing involving a 118 metre (323 ft) ascent to viewpoints above the Taw Valley.
Facilities: Pub in Umberleigh.

Leave the station car park and for a few yards head left along the B3227 in the direction of the river. Just before the bridge, turn left along a lane [SP Warkleigh] which leads past the post office with the River Taw immediately on the right. The lane later crosses the railway at one of the two level crossings along the Tarka Line equipped with automatic signals and requiring train drivers to observe speed restrictions. (The level crossings at Eggesford and Crediton, both staff operated, require the train to come to a complete halt.)

Once across the railway, follow the lane along the valley to the Brightley Cross intersection. Here continue ahead [SP Warkleigh]. After 0.2 miles be on the alert for a footpath sign pointing left past Toits Cottages. Take this path, which leads steeply up an ancient way between high earth banks to reach a gate and a field with barns. The footpath ends just beyond, where a lane executes a sharp corner. This is Brightley Barton, a 16th Century house with an earlier, mediaeval moat just left of the lane. The Devon historian, W.G. Hoskins, writing in the mid 20th Century,

Cross near Eastacott

observed disparagingly that the "house has been considerably pulled about." Note the mounting block, for easy access to a horse's saddle, by the front wall.

Proceed straight ahead and gently uphill along this lane (which in season offers a fine crop of wild strawberries) for a further 0.9 miles to Stone Cross, a road junction guarded by an ancient granite cross.

There are many such crosses in Devon and, depending on the location, they served a specific function. Those on open moorland usually marked an ancient *track*. Those in villages or in town market places often served as the *focal point for community* festivities, and have occasionally been pressed into service as a war memorial. Sometimes a cross marked the *boundary* of ecclesiastic or manorial land, its removal or interference qualifying as a capital offence. Wayside crosses sited at remote road junctions far from villages not infrequently served as a convenient location where, in the distant days before churches, the inhabitants of several neighbouring communities could assemble to receive the Communion sacrament from an itinerant

priest or friar. Such crosses can sometimes be identified by the presence of a horizontal *altar* stone at their base. [See, for example, Crediton: Walk 3.] Rarely, except when sited within a churchyard, do the crosses indicate a gravesite. Whatever its original function, *this* cross makes a good hilltop stopping place with splendid views north and south along the Taw valley.

Ignoring the side road to Eastacott, continue ahead [SP Chittlehampton] for 200 yards to a metalled farm track on the left just before a road junction. Take this turning which leads down to Pitt farm. Beyond the farm stand a wooden gate and stile leading into a plantation of conifers interspersed with birch and hazel. The path drops gently down to Pitt wood, a mass of primroses in the spring. Continue downhill through the wood to

reach a field and follow its right-hand edge down to a metal gate at the bottom end. Immediately beyond the gate lies the most rural of crossroads, with tracks leading left, right (up to North Nethercleave, formerly the West Country's only snail farm) and *straight ahead*. Take this third option along a grassy way bordered by high hedges to reach South Nethercleave. Here the path turns abruptly right and heads along a drive to pass a primary school. Just beyond, lies the B3227. Turn left onto the main road and, keeping a close eye on children and dogs, make your way over the railway bridge to Umberleigh station. The pub lies straight ahead on the far side of the river bridge. [*To avoid the main road: dog-leg right a few yards across the B3227 and take the footpath opposite to reach the river bank. Turn sharp left under the railway bridge and follow the riverside path to reach the village.*]

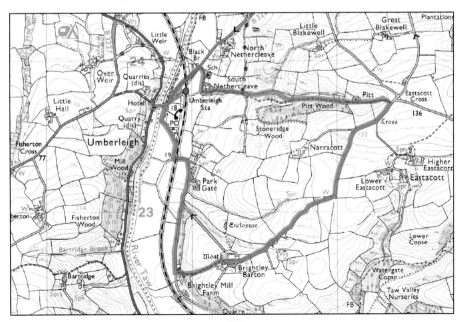

UMBERLEIGH

Walk 4. Cobbaton roller-coaster. 4.5 miles. 3.25 hours.
A walk to Cobbaton by a shorter (but no less scenic) route than Umberleigh: Walk 2,
for those wishing to spend extra time at the Combat Collection.
Outbound sections very muddy after rain. Wear appropriate footwear.
Facilities: Pub at Umberleigh. Museum, shop and refreshments at Cobbaton.
Museum open April through October. Closed Saturdays, except July & August.
For winter times call: (01769) 540740. Admission fee charged.

Leave the station car park and for a few yards head left along the B3227 towards the River Taw. Don't cross the bridge (note, however, the pub's location on the far bank, should it be required later!) but turn right along a signed footpath running past an antiques warehouse, formerly the premises of Murch Brothers, a well known North Devon agricultural engineering firm. The footpath follows the River Taw downstream, ducking under the railway at Black Bridge, and continuing over a footbridge and alongside the river for a further 0.4 miles, before veering away from the bank across a field (often with horses and muddy) to reach a stile leading to a quiet lane.

Your roller-coaster now begins. Turn left along the lane, your ascent rewarded by increasingly good views to the South along the Taw Valley. From the hilltop crossroads [Hawkridge Cross] several church towers are visible when not obscured by summer foliage: Atherington across the valley, High Bickington farther south and the massive Tudor tower of Chittlehampton 1.5 miles to the East. Dog-leg slightly left at the crossroads [SP Hawkridge] and descend to Hawkridge Brook.

Cross the stream but, 100 yards or so beyond the bridge where the lane bends left, continue straight ahead up an unsigned bridleway. Follow this undulating, often muddy and in places overgrown track for 0.8 miles. (Mud splatters and bramble scars acquired here will provide you with a suitably authentic look

when making your appearance at the Combat Collection!) Reaching a remote crossroads [Chuggaton Cross] turn right [SP Cobbaton] and, after 0.25 miles at an unsigned T-junction, right again. After 50 yards, at Lower Cobbaton Cross, continue ahead. The family-owned Cobbaton Combat Collection lies beyond on the left. Here amid the peace of the Devon countryside is an incredible array of military equipment, featuring some 45 vehicles (including working tanks) along with a vast assortment of weaponry. In season, a NAAFI truck offers simple refreshments. (**Note:** The stated duration of the walk does *not* take into account the time you spend here. Linger, and you may need to reconsider which train to take home.)

Follow the lane beyond the museum for a further 0.4 miles, keeping an eye out in the right-hand hedge for a footpath sign or, rather, *two* signs (evidence, no doubt, of a fiercely fought local skirmish!) Ignoring this footpath continue along the lane for a further 0.5

A local skirmish?

112

HIKE for HEALTH
SOUTHERN RAILWAY
Go-as-you-please cheap tickets
get you to the country quickest
Ask for details at any S-R Office and buy
'Southern Rambles' by S-P-B-Mais 6 d

DEVON (SR)

River Taw north of Umberleigh

where the bridleway is crossed by a footpath. Turn right and follow this pleasant path between high grassy banks to emerge at South Nethercleave Farm. Follow the farm entrance drive which bends right and continues past the village primary school to the B3227. Turn left along the main road and carefully make your way over the railway bridge to the station. The pub (that with military forethought you reconnoitred earlier) lies just over the river bridge.

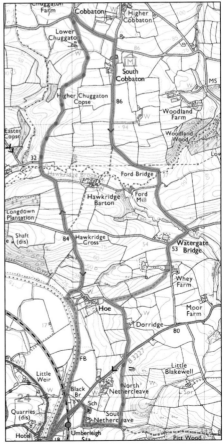

miles, crossing Ford Bridge and later arriving at a T-junction [Watergate Cross]. Turn right [SP Umberleigh], immediately recrossing Hawkridge Brook at Watergate Bridge, and proceed uphill to a fork. Keep left [SP Umberleigh] and, after 300 yards at the top of the hill, take a signed footpath on the right at the entrance to Whey Park. The view is superb. Pause and take your bearings. The footpath immediately leads left over a stile and across three fields. Set a course that keeps you on the *left-hand (south) side* of the little valley forming ahead and below you, aiming for a gate in the second field some 200 yards above the valley bottom. On the far side of a third field stands a stile leading into a lane. Turn left along this lane, passing several houses to reach a crossroads.

Cross with care and continue straight ahead along a bridleway for 0.2 miles, to a point

UMBERLEIGH

Walk 5. Warkleigh & Satterleigh. 8.4 miles. 5.5 hours.
A gentle beginning gives way to a stiff climb and a lengthy walk to visit a remote late-mediaeval gem perched on the peninsula separating the Taw & Mole valleys. Views to Exmoor and Dartmoor.
Facilities: Pub at Umberleigh. No pubs en route; take a snack.

Leave the station car park and head left along the B3227. Immediately before the river bridge, stay left along a road [SP Warkleigh] which heads upstream beside the Taw. Take the level crossing over the railway and continue up the valley to Brightley Cross. Here continue ahead [SP Warkleigh] for 1.3 miles of easy valley walking. At a sharp left-hand bend the lane abandons river and railway and heads steeply uphill (or, as William White put it 160 years ago, "rises boldly") for 0.4 miles to reach Shortridge Farm (with peacocks, so keep dogs under control) on the left. Just beyond, be alert for a footpath sign set back in the right-hand hedge. Take this path past Little Shortridge (noting the old well) and bear left uphill to a lane and across several fields to reach Warkleigh's isolated church of St. John.

Warkleigh parish is a union of two distinct entities: Warkleigh and Satterleigh (the latter, further east, having its own church, St. Peter's.) White, having "risen boldly" (on horseback, no doubt!) visited St. John's prior to 1850 and found "a handsome structure, with a tower and three bells." A century later, Devon's eminent historian W.G. Hoskins was less charitable: "A 15th, early 16th cent. building but over-restored and dull." The tower screen (using mid 16th Century carvings salvaged from a rood screen dismantled in 1850) is stunning.

From St. John's the footpath curves east under a massive oak before crossing a lane and following field edges (with views of distant Dartmoor's Cawsand Beacon) to reach a second lane. Cross this lane, and follow first a track and shortly a footpath on the right to reach

Warkleigh hamlet and its late-Victorian school-house on the far side of another lane. Turn left, descend to a stream and, just beyond at Warkleigh Cross, turn right [SP Satterleigh]. After 0.4 undulating miles, at Satterleigh Cross T-junction, bear right past Pearce & Dyers farm. At a gentle left-hand bend, take a signed footpath to the right leading to St. Peter's, Satterleigh. In Hoskins's view, "small, simple and charming, it is essentially a 15th cent. building with a wooden bell-cote." The south door, still in its original frame, is late-mediaeval. Note the wooden sounding board above the pulpit and the rows of 18th Century hat-pegs. In 1995 responsibility for the church passed to the Churches Conservation Trust, whose regulations permit six services a year. At the annual Rogation [prior to Ascension] Day service at Satterleigh Barton farm adjoining

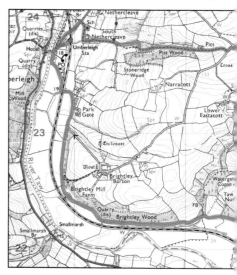

the church, the tiny congregation still follows in their ancestors' footprints, progressing round church and farm to "ask for God's blessing on all his creation," perhaps carrying bunches of milkwort, the sacred Rogation flower.

St. Peter's, Satterleigh

Immediately beyond St. Peter's, turn left past Satterleigh Barton and along its drive to reach a lane (noting the well by the left gatepost). Turn left and follow this lane (with South Molton visible to the East) for 0.9 miles past Pearce & Dyers and Hilltown to Hilltown Cross. Keep ahead [unsigned] for 0.2 miles, at East Pugsley Cross bearing left [SP Broadmoor] for a further 0.6 miles to West Pugsley Cross. Turn right [SP Chittlehampton] for 150 yards, then at Broadmoor Cross turn left [SP Eastacott] for 1.2 miles to Eastacott Cross. Turn left [SP Brightley], but after 50 yards turn right along a signed track leading down past Pitt Farm, over a stile and into a pleasant plantation.

The path continues downhill to Pitt Wood, and through the trees to a field. Follow its right-hand edge to the metal gate at the bottom. At the footpath crossroads just beyond stay ahead between high hedges to South Nethercleave. Bear right and follow its drive past the primary school to the B3227. Turn left onto this main road and exercise care as you make your way over the railway bridge to the station. The pub is just across the river.

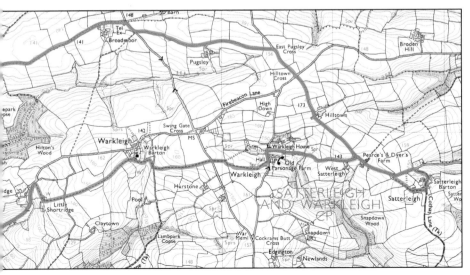

CHAPELTON

Newton St. Cyres and Chapelton, the first and last stops along the line, have something in common: minimal weekday train service and not too much of interest to greet the alighting passenger. Newton St. Cyres, to its credit, boasts an excellent trackside pub; Chapelton merely a sawmill. To compensate for these omissions, the scenery is delightful. The "down" platform remains in use, the former station house and the old "up" platform being sequestered behind a private fence. The station's early history was erratic. The "Taw Vale railway" line to Barnstaple opened to traffic in 1854, but no passenger facilities were available here until 1857 when the station opened as Chapel*town*. Just over three years later, it shut its doors for 15 years, reopening (as Chapel*ton*) in March 1875.

Walk 1. Chapelton to Umberleigh. One-way. 3.5 miles. 2.5 hours.
Apart from the first and last sections, this walk over the hills north-east of the River Taw is along quiet lanes, and may be tackled without difficulty after wet weather. Those in search of a more demanding day out may wish to combine this excursion with Umberleigh: Walk 1. -- a 7.6 mile round-trip.
Facilities: Pub at Umberleigh.

Leave the platform and make your way a few yards beyond its north (Barnstaple) end, where a footpath leads over the line. Cross with care and follow the path across a meadow to reach a well buttressed Victorian footbridge over the River Taw. (This, of course, is otter country. In freshwater habitats such as this, Tarka's descendents -- up to a yard long when fully grown -- typically have a territorial range of three to twelve miles. Living as they do at the top of the food chain, they have, apart from man, no natural predators and, barring accidents, enjoy a life expectancy of about five years.)

On the far bank, after 200 yards or so and just beyond a fine beech tree, the path divides. Take the left fork that leads over a stile and heads diagonally across a meadow to reach

a gate in the shade of a stand of ancient oak trees. Turn left into the lane running along the valley bottom to reach the tiny hamlet of Herner -- a church and little more. The church, or more correctly the chapel of ease, was erected in 1888. Some of the oak fittings to be found inside were transferred from the private chapel at Hall, the nearby seat of the Hall (later the Chichester) family.

At Herner Cross by the church, turn right [SP Cobbaton & Stowford] and in 0.4 miles, at Hill Cross, keep right [SP Kewsland & Emmett] and follow this lane for 1.25 miles. After passing Kewsland descend steeply to cross Hawkridge Brook, and continue up the other side to reach a crossroads [Hawkridge Cross]. Here, proceed straight ahead [SP Umberleigh] and steeply downhill. The view

of the Taw Valley is superb. At the bottom of the hill, where the lane bends left just before a small stream, take the signed footpath in the right-hand hedge. Follow the path, possibly muddy, over two stiles and down to the bank of the river, where the footpath bears left, upstream.

The pleasant riverside footpath continues over a footbridge and under the railway

bridge to reach Umberleigh. Murch Brothers, for many years a leading North Devon engineering company specialising in tractor work, is just to your right, though much of the firm's business these days seems to consist of lawn-mower repair. Part of the old premises now operates as an antiques warehouse. The station lies to your left, just a few yards up the B3227 towards South Molton.

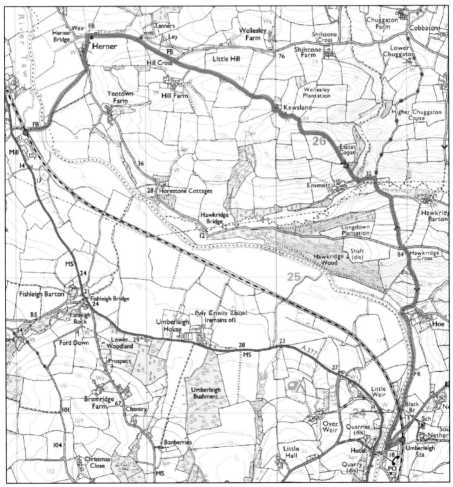

CHAPELTON

Walk 2. Herner and Hall. 4.6 miles. 2.5 hours.

A comparatively short walk which begins alongside the River Taw before climbing into the hills lying east of the valley. Take something to eat and drink. Not many of the walks in this series are without either pub or tearoom but this, alas, is an exception!

Facilities: None.

Leave the platform and make your way a few yards beyond its north (Barnstaple) end, where a footpath leads over the line. Cross carefully and follow the path across a meadow to reach a well buttressed Victorian footbridge over the River Taw. Almost certainly this bridge was erected to allow the Chichester family, the owners of Hall (the large house dominating the hill to the North) to reach the west bank of the river and the railway station. Note the "land arch" on the railway side of the bridge. When the river is in spate this reduces pressure on the bridge piers by providing an additional escape route for flood waters. On the far bank, after 200 yards or so, the

In the 1930s the prolific S.P.B. Mais wrote innumerable guides to Southern Railway destinations.

path divides just beyond a fine beech tree. Take the left fork that leads over a stile and heads diagonally across the meadow to reach a gate nestled beneath a stand of ancient oak trees. Turn left into the lane running along the valley bottom to reach the tiny hamlet of Herner. A private postern gate set in the wall opposite the late 19th Century chapel of ease leads directly up to Hall, the local "big" house.

From the chapel, head west [SP New Bridge & Barnstaple] back in the direction of the river along a lane which almost immediately turns right at Herner Bridge. Just as you reach the woods of Hall, turn right at a footpath sign. Climb over a stile and follow the drive uphill. The house is still in private ownership; keep dogs securely leashed and pay careful attention to all footpath signs. From a distance Hall could possibly pass for Tudor, but was actually rebuilt in the mid-19th Century by Robert Chichester in the Elizabethan style that was then in vogue. A similar style was adopted for the rebuilding of ill-fated Creedy Park, near Crediton, early in the last century.

The footpath leads past Hall's walled garden, several outbuildings (some of which clearly predate the house itself) and a grain store. Sadly, the rear section of the main house has been allowed to fall into disrepair. The route then follows the back drive uphill. Note the fine stone well 100 yards distant in a field to the left and the sunken well-house in the bank on the right. At the top of the hill the back

drive emerges from the Hall estate at a right-angled lane bend.

Proceed straight ahead for a few yards before taking a signed turning on the right leading past Lower Woolstone farm entrance and then along a track. This descends (past evidence of extensive pheasant rearing) to a stream, before continuing onwards and upwards for a further 0.5 miles to reach Upcott Farm at the top of the rise. In late April the wildflowers -- primroses, violets and bluebells -- can be spectacular as you trudge up the hill.

At last the track emerges onto a very minor lane. Turn right to pass between the farm and Upcott Cottage, and then immediately bear left to follow the public road gently downhill. At the first T-junction, turn right to reach Shilstone Cross. Here, turn right again and follow the road for 1.2 miles, past Hill Cross and down the hill into Herner.

Hall and its chapel

Turn left at the chapel and after 0.1 miles retrace your steps along the footpath and back over the River Taw to reach the station.

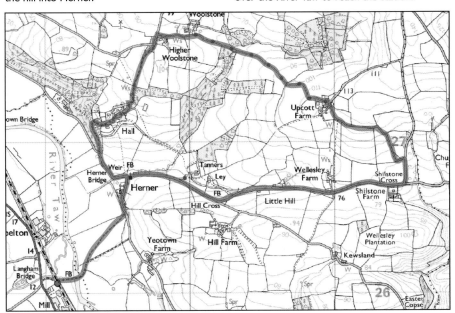

CHAPELTON

Walk 3. Beneath Watchful Skies: Hildrew, Harracott & Heccaton.
4.3 miles. 2.25 hours.
A peaceful walk, mostly along quiet lanes and bridleways.
Expect mud along the section between Week and Hildrew. Wear appropriate footwear.
No refreshments; take a picnic.
Facilities: None.

Leave the platform and make your way to its north (Barnstaple) end. Here a path leads left alongside a river to the old Exeter-Barnstaple turnpike road (now the A377). Turn right to face the oncoming traffic, and with *great care* make your way across Langham Lake, a tributary of the Taw, here celebrating its final moments of independent identity. A converted Victorian chapel lies some 250 yards beyond the river bridge on the opposite side of the road. At this chapel [Chapelton Cross], turn left into a quiet lane [SP Ensis and Hiscott].

Tarka (aka *Lutra lutra*, the European River Otter)

© Pat Morris

and by a more impressive structure: another converted Victorian chapel, tucked behind trees a stone's throw away in the north-east quadrant. Keep ahead [SP Hiscott] along the lane which gradually descends to a little valley and the tiny hamlet of Heccaton. Blink and you'll miss it! At Heccaton Bridge T-junction, immediately before the river, turn right along a very minor lane [SP Week].

After passing Heccaton on your left, some 150 yards further on where the lane veers right, stay to the left along an unsigned bridleway, which ascends the east side of the little valley for 0.2 miles before emerging at a bend in a lane. Turn right into the lane and follow it for 0.2 miles to arrive at a crossroads.

Follow the lane gently uphill along the north side of the Langham Lake valley for 0.6 miles to a sharp left-hand turn by Hildrew Farm. Continue along the lane past a succession of bends to an intersection directly opposite Sweetfield East. Stay straight ahead here, passing Harracott House, a Georgian residence, and continue to Ensis Cross. The intersection is presided over by Harracott Village Hall

Turn left here [SP Week] immediately entering Harracott, a larger community than Heccaton. At first sight, you may think there's not very much to this quiet hamlet, beyond a couple of picturesque thatched cottages, several

conversions, a scattering of modern houses and a notice board (which in 2009 was still advertising events that had taken place nine years earlier.) Harracott, it turns out, is no stranger to time warp and any sense you now have of rural seclusion may be entirely illusory. Indeed it is quite possible, as you peer at the notice board, that you are under alien observation. For in December 2000, a "silver, cigar-shaped object, moving faster than a nearby plane" was observed in the skies directly overhead.

Lacking any invitation to step aboard something cigar-shaped, continue through the hamlet, keeping straight ahead [SP Week] at the intersection located at the hamlet's further end. After 0.4 miles, at an intersection [Harracott Cross] turn left to arrive at Higher Week Farm and, just beyond, a T-junction. Bear right here [SP Week] and follow the lane for 300 yards to an unsigned crossroads. Turn right down the least travelled of the four lanes, and prepare yourself for a section of the walk that's decidedly down to earth. Beyond the last house, with electric entrance gates and a

wall intercom reminiscent of suburban Surrey, the route rapidly degenerates. Chapelton: Walk 3. annually competes with Morchard Road: Walk 1. for the coveted title of "Muddiest Tarka Line Walk". Consider yourself duly warned as you follow an overgrown footpath that dog-legs left and gradually descends to Hildrew Bridge, though by early autumn the bridge is completely concealed by dense foliage.

London and South Western Ry.
TO
CHAPELTON

Continue, equally gently, up the south side of the valley to reach Hildrew Farm, joining a metalled road at the farm's farther side. Walk straight ahead along the road [SP Chapelton] for 0.6 miles to return to the chapel beside the A377. Turn right and *exercise care* as you make your way back over Langham Bridge to the station, immediately to your left on the far side of the river.

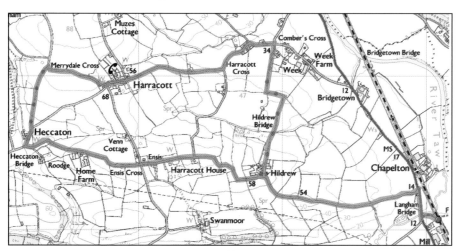

CHAPELTON

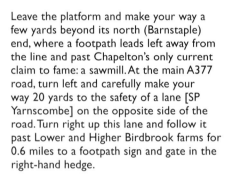

Walk 4. Yarnscombe. 5.8 miles. 3.5 hours.
The remote landscape between the Taw and Torridge is very much Tarka country and offers splendid views and some stiff climbs. Take something to eat and drink; this walk, unfortunately, features neither pub nor tearoom.
Facilities: None.

Leave the platform and make your way a few yards beyond its north (Barnstaple) end, where a footpath leads left away from the line and past Chapelton's only current claim to fame: a sawmill. At the main A377 road, turn left and carefully make your way 20 yards to the safety of a lane [SP Yarnscombe] on the opposite side of the road. Turn right up this lane and follow it past Lower and Higher Birdbrook farms for 0.6 miles to a footpath sign and gate in the right-hand hedge.

Follow this footpath across three fields to Langley Barton. Pass just to the right of a modern barn, and left through a gate before an older cob-walled barn to reach a lane. Turn right past the front of the property. The present house dates from the early 17th Century, but its core is much older. The original building was a five-bay cross-passage barton house. A room to the right of the old cross passage has a stone in the fireplace bearing the date 1624 and the initials R.P., probably referring to Richard Pollard whose family resided in Langley from 1303 to 1732. One of the Langley Pollards was Court Usher both to Elizabeth I and her successor, James I. The Pollard coat of arms may be seen above the front door. The property is flanked by ancient outbuildings.

Follow the lane down to Langley Bridge. A spindleberry, now fairly rare but one of at least three to be spotted on this walk, on the stream's farther bank produces red berries in October. Buck's Mill, a corn mill named after a Squire Buck, a prosperous merchant

with several such mills on his wide-ranging properties, lies beyond the bridge. The mill was originally powered by an overshot wheel requiring an especially long leat. Proceed steeply uphill for 0.2 miles to a footpath in the left-hand hedge. Take this path which forges uphill along a succession of right-hand field edges. Note the overgrown lane just below and to your right along which the grain was once brought down to Buck's Mill. At Ley Farm, the former home of a Langley Barton tenant farmer (note the Pollard coat of arms on the building's south face), turn left and follow a lane uphill to Yarnscombe.

Remote from both railway and main roads, the village, mentioned in the Domesday Book as "Hernescombe, valley of the eagles," retains a peaceful feel. William White's list of the village's population in 1850 is instructive. In addition to 22 farmers and the curate, he records there being one carpenter, one mason, a smithy, two shoemakers, two tailors, one victualler and the rather intriguing "Tout Grace, beer seller." (Male or female we know not!) In other words, very much the rural basics with farmers slaughtering their own livestock and baking being done at home. Press on past a converted chapel to St. Andrew's church, which has Norman beginnings. Its superb 13th Century granite pillars were very probably dragged from Dartmoor on sledges. The south aisle and porch were added in the 15th Century. The sundial above the porch was installed in 1788 by John Berry, who was responsible also for the famed sundial at Tawstock. [See Barnstaple: Walk 4.]

From the church retrace your steps to the intersection just before the converted chapel. Turn left [SP "Unsuitable for Motors"] and follow this road for 200 yards, before turning right along a well-signed footpath. The path crosses two fields, passes along a green way and then follows field edges down to a stream and footbridge, before climbing steeply to Cleave Farm. Here cross a final stile and turn right along the farm's drive to reach a lane. Bear right, downhill, continuing ahead both at Rooks Cross and at the next intersection.

At Bustley Bridge, turn left [SP Ensis] over the stream and climb steeply up the far bank to reach Ensis Cross and its isolated Victorian chapel half hidden in the north-east quadrant. Turn right [SP Chapelton] past the village hall and follow the northern side of the Langham Lake valley gently downhill. Continue for 1.2 miles to the main road. Turn right at Chapelton Cross along the busy A377. Face the oncoming traffic taking *particular care* of children and dogs. The station lies 250 yards ahead on the left just beyond Langham Bridge.

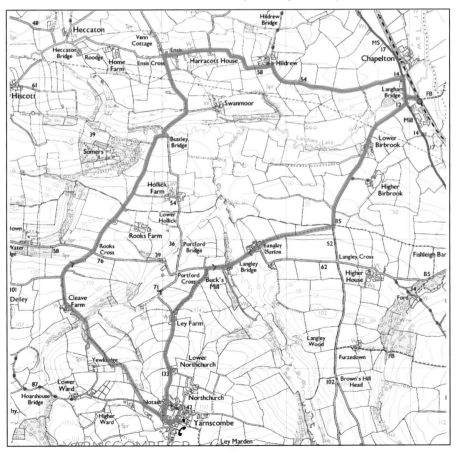

BARNSTAPLE

Located on the Taw Estuary, Barnstaple has been a place of importance since Saxon times. Like Bideford on the Torridge, Barnstaple's name and location was probably determined by the fact that this was the first place the Taw could safely be forded, a post or *stapol* marking the spot, hence the name "*Bearda's staple*". Castle mound is all that remains of a fortress probably erected by William I. In mediaeval times a flourishing woollen manufacturing and export industry ensured Barnstaple's prosperity. In terms of importance it ranks as the third town in Devon, after Exeter and Plymouth, a position it has held since the 14th Century. Efforts are currently afoot to promote Barnstaple as the "Gateway" to North Devon.

Walk 1. The Banks of the Taw. 2 miles. 1.25 hours.
This, the shortest walk in the series, is full of historical interest. A stroll across Barnstaple's ancient Long Bridge is followed by a gentle upstream amble along the river bank. The return route, which crosses the river on a disued railway bridge, is equally undemanding.
Facilities: Stationmaster's Café, Barnstaple Platform 1 (closes early p.m. Saturdays, & all day on Sunday). Superstore three minutes' walk. Pubs and cafés in the town.

© Bob Small Photography

Barnstaple's Long Bridge

From the platform take Station Road towards the town centre, passing B&Q on your left and Tesco away to your right. At the roundabout bear right to reach Barnstaple's famous Long Bridge. Constructed around 1280, the bridge has had an eventful life. First repaired in 1333, it was partially destroyed in both 1437 and 1646, and duly rebuilt on each occasion. Road widening took place in 1796 and additional widening work was undertaken between 1832 and 1834. The latter improvements were directed by Devon's first County Bridge Surveyor, James Green, former assistant to John Rennie and an acknowledged expert, who 20 years earlier had built the graceful three-arch bridge over the waters of the Exe and Creedy at Cowley [See Exeter: Walk 2.] The post-war boom in vehicle ownership put further pressure on Barnstaple's historic structure, which was widened yet again in 1963. The 1989 opening of the new bridge,

0.4 miles downstream, reduced the Long Bridge's work-load, but the ancient structure remains architecturally sound and its retirement is not contemplated.

As you glance over the Long Bridge parapet, it is immediately apparent from the muddy banks that here, as it nears salt water, the Taw is tidal. In 1850 William White observed that "the river is navigable for barges and small craft to about three miles above the town," but long before White the gradual accumulation of sand and mud in the Taw estuary had silted up Barnstaple's harbour and led to the town's commercial undoing. Inexorably Barnstaple's foreign trade passed to Bideford where, as Devon historian W.G. Hoskins noted, "the more powerful tidal currents of the Torridge … kept the deep-water channel clear," reducing Barnstaple's once proud commercial activity to the smaller vessels required for coastal trading.

The view downstream was not always as you see it now. Not only have the ocean-going sailing ships long since departed from Barnstaple's Castle Quay, but a curving iron railway bridge just yards down-river connected "Barnstaple Junction" (the existing "Barnstaple" station by which you arrived) with "Barnstaple Town", the town-centre station on the northern bank, from which trains continued on to the seaside resort of Ilfracombe. This railway bridge, completed in 1874, was dismantled in 1977 after Beeching's axe severed the Ilfracombe branch. (There's general agreement that the view from Long Bridge has greatly improved with its removal!)

At the far end of Long Bridge turn right past Barnstaple's excellent museum, and follow Taw Vale road upstream alongside the river. When this road veers inland at Rock Park, continue by the Taw for a further 0.4 miles. Beyond a sports field on the left, an iron

bridge spans the river. This marks the former route of a GWR spur line, constructed in 1887 to connect "Barnstaple Junction" with South Molton, Taunton and on to Paddington, Cardiff & the Midlands. As late as August 1960, this bridge on a Saturday was carrying 13 "up" departures to Taunton and beyond. (An additional 12 "up" trains took the rival L&SW -- later the Southern Railway -- route, remaining south of the river on today's Tarka Line, bound for King's Nympton, Yeoford, Exeter and, seven times out of the dozen, Waterloo.) On the final summer weekends before mass motor-car ownership, the West Country railway lines were still doing bumper business!

Climb up to the bridge, and cross to the farther bank. Descend and follow the riverside path back to Long Bridge. If the children are tired or you're in need of a short-cut, B&Q and the railway station may later be glimpsed across a car park to your left.

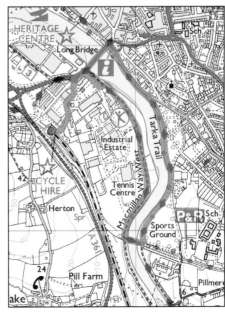

BARNSTAPLE

From the platform take Station Road towards the town centre passing B&Q on your left and Tesco away to your right. At the roundabout bear right towards the river. Just before Barnstaple's famous Long Bridge, turn right along a path [Cycle Route 3] heading upstream between Seven Brethren Bank and the Taw. Pause for a moment to observe the 13th Century bridge with its 15 pointed masonry arches.

Continue upstream keeping to the river bank. After 0.6 miles a disused railway bridge over the Taw marks the former route of a GWR spur line linking "Barnstaple Junction" (the station by which you arrived) with Taunton, London and the Midlands. Leave the cycle route, continuing under this bridge and alongside the river. The distinctive tower crowning the hill to your right was erected in the 18th Century by Lord Wrey of Tawstock Court as a lookout from which to view his estate. (A firm of accountants has now taken possession.)

Peaceful waterside walking next takes you beneath the bypass linking the A39 with the A361. Continue through the land arch (flooded when the Taw is in spate) beneath the Tarka Line to a wood above a side-stream. There's a little scrambling here as you leave the river to follow this stream, but the trail is marked by wooden posts.

Emerging from the trees, cross a field and turn left over the stile to join a quiet lane. Once beyond crenellated Shorleigh Bridge head steeply uphill (through, of all things, a tunnel) and over the brow to the picturesque village of Tawstock.

At the first fork keep left [SP *cul de sac* & church] and left again round a corner past the hound-topped gateposts (the iron gates are gone) marking the entrance to Tawstock Court (until 2012 the site of St. Michael's School). If you have plenty of time to catch that rare commodity -- a train willing to stop at Chapelton -- the church of St. Peter beyond Tawstock Court has one of the finest collections of memorial monuments in England, and fully justifies a visit. [Please see Barnstaple: Walk 4 for further details.] Well before the Tudor gatehouse (1574), opposite the old estate sawmills, double back along a footpath on your right leading through a pleasant beech wood above the village.

Follow this footpath for 0.3 miles, past an overgrown quarry on the left and through metal gates leading straight across the upper farmyard of Park Gate with its large modern barn. Ignoring other options, keep alongside the next two right-hand hedges that lie beyond to join a lane. Turn left to reach Smemington Cross [formerly Lodge Corner], and here keep right [SP Harracott].

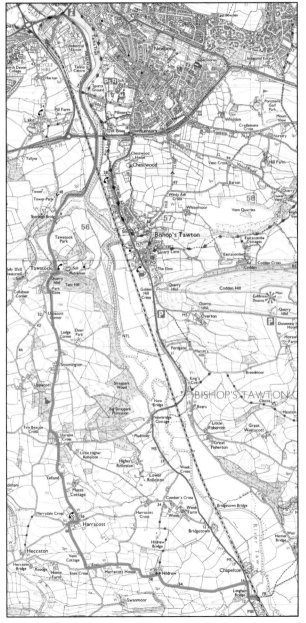

A seemingly endless uphill drag now begins, past Oak Farm to reach Uppacott Wood Nature Reserve just before the brow. At the road fork beyond keep left, shortly reaching the splendidly named Harepie Cross. Continue ahead [SP Harracott] and downhill -- rewarded for your recent labours by the view that now opens up across the Langham Lake (a *river*, there is no lake) valley -- for 0.6 miles to enter Harracott village. Turn right at the Harracott T-junction and walk up through the little community to its farther end, where the road splits into three.

Here turn sharp left [SP Village Hall], and after 0.4 miles at Ensis Cross where an old chapel has been converted to a spectacular private house, turn left [SP Chapelton] past the less than spectacular village hall. Follow the northern side of the valley mostly downhill for 1.2 miles, passing Hildrew on the left, to reach the main road. Turn right [Chapelton Cross] onto the busy A377. Face the oncoming traffic taking particular care of children and dogs before crossing over to the station approach lane, 250 yards ahead on the left just beyond Langham Bridge.

BARNSTAPLE

Walk 3. Back of Beyond -- the Western Hamlets. 8.5 miles. 5.5 hours.
The longest walk in the series, and a varied one. The bustle of Barnstaple gives
way to a level stroll beside the Taw, followed by more demanding walking along
the peaceful lanes of a bygone era.
Facilities: Barnstaple: Stationmaster's Café (closed early p.m. Saturdays, & all day
Sundays); Superstore three minutes' walk. Café at Fremington Quay.
Pubs & shops at Fremington.

Cross over at the pedestrian traffic lights outside the station entrance and turn left. At all fingerposts follow directions via Cycle Path 3 to Bideford. Decorated subways burrow beneath two roads in succession emerging at a disused railway track running alongside the south bank of the river.

Until the 1960s the elevated track-bed along which you're now walking connected "Barnstaple Junction" with Bideford, Torrington and onwards via Hatherleigh to Halwill Junction (for Bude, Padstow or Okehampton). The track was taken up in 1985. The route briefly re-opened 24 years later for an attempt by television presenter James May to send a 00-gauge *model* train on the ten-mile run to Bideford -- a project that, sadly, succumbed to vandalism and electrical problems.

Soon the Taw loops away to the North-west for a mile or so. Ahead across the estuary Heanton Punchardon's church tower is clearly visible. After entering a primrose-filled cutting with a bridge and, beyond, a "W" [whistle] sign, the track rejoins the river at Fremington Quay, formerly a landing place for freight and coal, with its own railway station (now a café). To the North across the Taw is Chivenor airfield, well known for its search & rescue work.

Beyond the Quay is an inlet -- the Fremington Pill. Once across, turn immediately left [Route 33] up the Pill's west bank along a footpath leading to

Fremington. The village was once famed for its clay, much of it transported between 1450 and 1540 to potteries in Barnstaple to make the embossed floor tiles gracing many a West- or North-Devon church. Just before the main road on your right stands Fremington Manor, a very fine 18th Century house, remodelled in the 1880s by the Yeo family and now a care home.

The New Inn, conveniently, stands just across the B3233 on the corner of Old School Lane. Once refreshed, continue south down this lane. Beyond the last houses, at Picketts Gate, keep left and 0.2 miles further on, just past a cemetery on the right, turn left onto an unsigned lane leading steadily uphill to Kari Koa (hardly a Devon name!) and Horsacott Farm. A few hundred yards beyond the farm and its barn conversions, a lane from the right joins yours immediately before a T-junction [Myrtle Cottage]. Turn left for 100 yards before taking a lane on the right [SP *Cul-de-sac*] leading under the A39 and uphill to Lower and Higher Rookabear. Beyond the latter the lane reverts to a muddy hilltop track, a mass of wildflowers in spring, before emerging at Nottiston Cross. Dog-leg five yards left and proceed straight ahead, following the lane round a sharp left-hand bend to pass Nottiston farm. Codden Hill across the Taw valley looms ahead as you walk the remaing yards to the little hamlet of St. John's Chapel.

Continue over the main road and downhill.

128

At the Eastacombe fingerpost, keep ahead to reach a chapel, beyond which on the right is a disused quarry. The fine hilltop views continue until your descent towards Tawstock. At Collabear Corner, keep left to reach the thatched schoolhouse. Immediately beyond, at a footpath sign, detour a few yards left to the restored (in 1938) Holy Well -- one of the grandest of more than 200 to be found in Devon. Continue uphill along the road through the pretty village. Tawstock church is justly famous for its wealth of memorials -- one of the finest collections in England. [See Barnstaple: Walk 4. for further details.]

Bear left [SP Barnstaple] at all turns as you climb the hill. Just over the crest, there's a surprise: a 19th Century tunnel over which the estate traffic of nearby Tawstock Court could pass unhindered. The route remains something of a roller-coaster for the final leg to Barnstaple. At the top of the next hill, note the tower on the left -- an 18th Century folly from which Lord Wrey could conveniently view his Tawstock estate. After crossing the A39 the lane enters the little hamlet of Lake before tackling a final hill and descending to a roundabout. Take the steps on the right and at the bottom turn right, under a bridge, to reach the station.

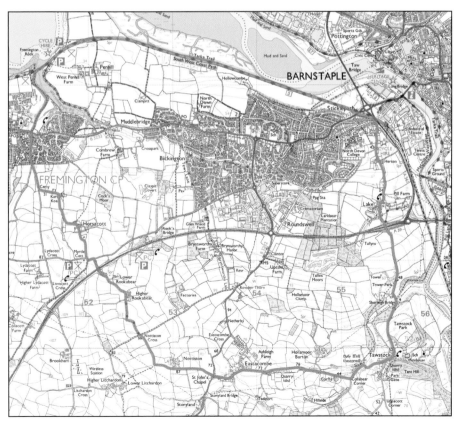

BARNSTAPLE

Exit the station, and turn left to the pedestrian traffic lights. Cross to the farther side, and turn left to walk under the road bridge. Immediately beyond, take the flight of steps leading up the left bank to a roundabout. Turn left up unsigned Sticklepath ("*steep path*") Hill.

Follow this road past Sticklepath Court and Herton to reach the small hamlet of Lake. Shortly beyond, the lane crosses over the A39 and provides good views of a tower on the right that has taken the name "Tawstock House". It was originally built by Lord Wrey in the 18th

Tawstock House

Century as a lookout from which to view the huge estate that you are about to enter. At the next dip in the road note the footpath on the left (your eventual route home) just before Shorleigh Bridge. Cross this and ascend the hill beyond, passing through a tunnel to reach Tawstock. At the first fork keep left [SP *cul de sac* & church] and left again round the corner. Tawstock Court, the large estate to your left, had its own sawmills and stables which you now pass. St. Michael's preparatory school relocated

here from Uxbridge during World War II and occupied the site until 2012.

The property has ancient and noble roots, being successively owned by the Brewer, Tracey, Martyn, Audley, Fitzwarren, Hankford and Bourchier families. The eldest daughter of Edward Bourchier, Earl of Bath, carried it in marriage to Sir Chichester Wrey, who was created a baronet in 1628. The house nearly burned down in 1787, but was soon afterwards rebuilt by Sir Bourchier Wrey to his own "Gothick" design. W.G. Hoskins, the 20th Century Devon historian, describes the rebuilt house in scathing terms: "remarkably ugly ... hideous." Others have taken a more charitable view, White in 1850 describing the rebuilt property as "a large and handsome mansion, delightfully situated in an extensive and well-wooded park ... near the line of the intended Taw Vale railway." ("Our" Tarka Line -- thought of, but not yet born!) The massive Tudor gateway (1574) is all that remains of the Bourchiers' original house.

Continue past the former school and down through the park to St. Peter's church, the focal point of the walk. In Hoskins's view "it contains one of the finest collections of monuments in Devon, and one of the most notable in England ... An entire half-day should be allowed for their inspection." The church structure has an unusual (for Devon) cruciform ground plan with a central tower and dates almost entirely from the early 14th Century. The gallery leading to the belfry may have been a minstrels' gallery

HIKE for HEALTH
SOUTHERN RAILWAY
Go-as-you-please cheap tickets
get you to the country quickest

Ask for details at any S-R Office and buy
"Southern Rambles" by S-P-B-Mais 6 d

DEVON (SR)

rescued from the manor after the 1787 fire, or may have been originally installed in 1697 in the west end of the nave and moved to its present position in 1867. The stunning Wrey manorial pew opposite the gallery is French Renaissance work and "perhaps the finest example of its kind in Devon." There are "green men" carved in both stone and wood and some exceptionally fine carved bench-ends.

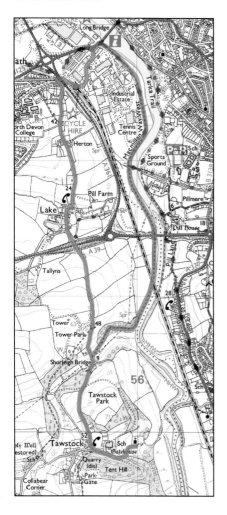

The earliest monument -- a 14th Century wooden effigy to an unknown lady has been moved to the safety of Barnstaple Museum, but the beautiful mural monument with a kneeling figure commemorating Mary St. John (1631) remains. Inside the altar rails stands a superb, sumptuously coloured tomb with the recumbent figures of both William Bourchier, 3rd Earl of Bath (d.1623) and Elizabeth, his wife, attended in death by their kneeling sons and daughters. There are numerous other notable memorial monuments throughout the building and, as Hoskins says, to inspect them adequately would take an afternoon.

On your way out, note the fine sundial above the south porch -- erected in 1757 and the work of John Berry -- which functions as a world clock providing the time in such places as Babilon & Samarcand [sic]. Berry's work may also be seen at Yarnscombe. [See Chapelton: Walk 4.] Unsurprisingly, the Bourchiers' sphere of influence could be found on both sides of the altar rails. When Sir Bouchier Palk Wrey (St. Peter's patron) was presiding over Tawstock Court in the mid 19th Century, he appointed as rector The Revd. Henry Bourchier Wrey, M.A. -- one of no fewer than five Bourchier family members to have held the living!

After you've had your fill of St. Peter's, return to the intersection, and take the road by which you entered the village through the tunnel (probably a 19th Century construction to allow the noble lords to visit all parts of the estate without coming into contact with lesser mortals!) and down the hill. Just after crossing Shorleigh Bridge, take the signed footpath on the right, which leads above a stream and through a wood to emerge on the west bank of the Taw. The riverside path then continues downstream under railway, road and (disused) railway bridges until it reaches Barnstaple's famous Long Bridge. Turn left and follow signs to the station.

BARNSTAPLE

Walk 5. Ashford & Bradiford. 6.3 miles. 3.75 hours.
The easy outbound route follows the former Southern Railway line towards Ilfracombe, the salt air along the Taw's tidal estuary giving city children a foretaste of the seaside holiday ahead. Fine views.
Facilities: Stationmaster's Café, Barnstaple Platform 1 [closed early p.m. Saturdays, & all day Sundays]. Superstore three minutes' walk. Pub at Bradiford. Pubs, cafés and shops in Barnstaple.

Take Station Road towards Barnstaple town centre. Bear right at the roundabout to cross the Long Bridge over the Taw. On the far, downstream side immediately descend steps and turn right along the Coast Path [Cycle Rt. 27 Braunton] along the river's north bank. Pass the old bus station, a signal box and through what was once Barnstaple Town railway station to reach Castle Quay. Three centuries ago, before the silting up of the river, the Quay would have been bustling with activity.

The path heads over a tributary of the Taw celebrating its final seconds before merging with the main river. This side-stream is yet *another* River Yeo (the *third* so named that we've encountered on these walks.) Unlike its namesakes, *this* Yeo had a solid *commercial* function. At high-tide vessels of up to 250 tonnes could navigate the channel, and quays were built upstream on both sides of the tributary to handle a coastal trade which at one time included coal shipped by water from South Wales. The Ilfracombe line crossed the Yeo on the Pottington Swing Bridge. This rotated horizontally to provide shipping with access to the wharves that lined both banks. Just beyond the river, a siding headed up the Yeo's west bank to service warehouses along Rolles Quay.

Pass under the the A361 bypass (opened 1989) and follow the coastal path for the next two miles. At low tide note the vast quantities of mud and sand that in recent centuries have accumulated in the Taw estuary, putting paid forever to Barnstaple's earlier prominence as a port and leaving the river to the gulls, Canada geese and oystercatchers. As the town's commercial fortunes declined, its rival Bideford -- blessed with more powerful tidal currents -- was in a position to capture much of Barnstaple's water-borne trade.

Speaking of rivalry, trains such as the Atlantic Coast Express were divided at Barnstaple Junction, the front portion following "our" track to Ilfracombe and the rear portion, bound for Fremington [See Barnstaple: Walk 3], Bideford and Torrington, following the south shore of the estuary. The Ilfracombe departure from Barnstaple Town coincided with the Torrington departure from Barnstaple Junction, with the result that the two trains appeared to race each other along north and south banks!

About 80 yards after passing under a stone bridge (leading to waterside limekilns), *duck left along an unsigned footpath* which doubles back over the bridge and up to the A361. Dog-leg right for 20 yards and cross with care to follow Limekiln Lane steeply uphill. The estuary views are spectacular. Just before Charlesworth turn right along a signed footpath leading across two fields to a lane. Turn right and follow this lane past a Gospel Chapel to an intersection [Tophill]. Turn right, downhill, into Ashford. Note the colour of the cob walls. The grey culm measures soil differs markedly from the red

Permian sandstone used for cob around, say, Yeoford. Make for St. Peter's church. Almost entirely rebuilt in 1854 (the year the railway reached Barnstaple), much of its 16th Century woodwork was re-used by the architect. The font is Norman.

From Rectory Cross, below the church, follow Strand Lane downhill for 80 yards, and turn left into Long Lane. After this heads downhill *fork left* along Higher New Close Lane and, after 150 yards at the next footpath fork, *stay left*. For the next 0.8 miles your route leads across fields. Immediately beyond Beara Cottage farm in its stately grove, descend to the farm drive. Cross this and another field to reach a stile and a stream. Continue across two meadows (with a folly crowning the hill to your right) to a road.

Turn right along this road into Bradiford. At the top of the hill beyond the pub stands the megalithic Pilton Longstone. Just before reaching it duck right into Chaddiford Lane and immediately left along a footpath that soon bears left above a school. At the path's far end, turn left and, at the next T-junction, right into Abbey Road. At the T-junction at its far end, keep ahead along a footpath leading beside the River Yeo. Before the footbridge, turn right along Mills Way. At the Rolle Street T-junction turn left. Cross the inner ring road into [No Entry/Pedestrians Only] Barnstaple High Street. The ancient Pannier Market and Butchers' Row are half way along on the left. Just beyond stands St. Peter's church with its twisted spire (re-leaded in 1636). At the High Street's farther end, retrace your steps over the Long Bridge to the station.

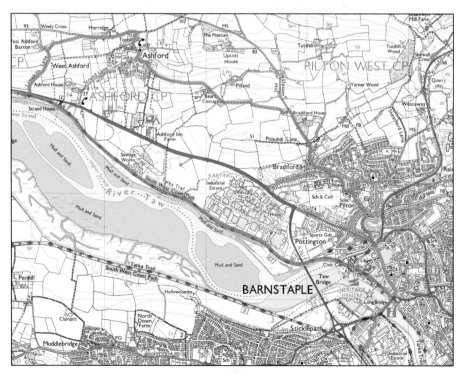

133

AFTERWORD

TO MORCHARD ROAD: "ONE CHILD, UNACCOMPANIED"

On summer afternoons the old station buildings at Morchard Road cast a long shadow, and in that shadow stands a blue metal bench. Sitting on this bench, awaiting the rattle of the diesel unit and contemplating the rampant vegetation across the track, my mind wanders back to the distant days when I first knew the station more than 60 years ago.

I was a commuter. Not a daily, weekly or even monthly commuter, but a commuter none the less. One who every summer from the age of six made the annual pilgrimage from London back to the well-remembered house near Morchard Bishop. The journey was essentially a home-coming -- to spend the summer holidays with my two great aunts with whom I'd been billeted during the latter years of the war -- and I doubt if any demobbed serviceman anticipated the journey with more joy than I.

There were, as there are today, essentially two routes: the Great Western Railway from Paddington to Exeter St. David's (convenient if the great aunts had an Exeter appointment with their chiropodist) or the Southern Railway's "through service" all the way to Morchard Road's little platform.

To compete with the GWR's "Cornish Riviera" and "Torbay Express", Southern also offered its Devon customers two named

A Bulleid Light Pacific approaches Morchard Road with a Waterloo-bound service, August 1958.

expresses. The all-Pullman "Devon Belle", alas, never stopped at Morchard Road, and extracted from its passengers a hefty fare supplement. After much pleading, I was permitted to take it just once, in the early '50s, returning to London from Exeter Central in the luxury of the Belle's rear "observation saloon" (in actual fact, a converted First World War hospital coach).

The second was Southern's "Atlantic Coast Express", the ACE -- a name dreamed up by F. Rowland, a guard from Great Torrington, who won a company-wide competition to name the train and was rewarded with a prize of three guineas for his pains. The ACE left London Waterloo every morning at 11:00 on the dot, and it was into this train that I would be deposited one summer morning around the end of July for the long journey west. In the very early years of unaccompanied travel, my mother insisted (much to my

mortification) that I be labelled like a suitcase, and no doubt the guard would be notified of my presence and slipped half a crown to keep an eye on me.

Boarding the ACE was not as simple as it sounds for, in an attempt to be all things to all men, the Southern Railway divided and sub-divided the train at several points along its route into as many as nine separate sections. Two slip coaches were dropped at Sidmouth Junction, one for Sidmouth and one for Exmouth (via Budleigh Salterton). At Exeter Central the train was divided into two halves. The front portion set off via "Yeoford Junction" for Okehampton, where the train was again split -- one section being destined for Tavistock and Plymouth, and the remaining carriages routed to Halwill Junction, to be subdivided into portions respectively serving Bude and Padstow. Five minutes after the departure of this front section from Exeter Central, the remaining coaches followed in their sisters' tracks as far as Coleford, before continuing along what is now the Tarka Line to Barnstaple Junction, where further separations -- to Torrington, Bideford and Ilfracombe -- occurred.

A minefield if ever there was one, for it was never a question of just climbing aboard the ACE at Waterloo, but climbing aboard the *correct portion* of the train. I don't believe I ever took the summer journey without seeing bewildered passengers having to leap out at Salisbury or Exeter Central in search of the specific coaches assigned to their eventual destination.

As we progressed, there was a pleasant sense of the train adjusting to its rural surroundings. Having started out at Waterloo in a carriage located in approximately the middle of a 12- or even 13-coach express, by the time we clattered into Crediton we were down to no more than four or five coaches.

All this, of course, could be closely monitored by an excited little boy in grey shorts and stockings clutching a grubby and much dog-eared train-spotter's book. The windows of the corridor train were secured with the aid of a long leather strap, and could be opened at passengers' convenience. Above each window was pasted a sign announcing that "it is dangerous to lean out of the window." I always interpreted this sign in its most literal sense, accepting that while it might indeed be dangerous to *lean* out, it was perfectly acceptable to put just my head out into the streaming airflow in order to monitor our westward progress.

Pleasures must be paid for, and as often as not I ended up, like innumerable children on innumerable trains, with a speck of coal dust from the engine firmly wedged beneath my reddening eye-lid. These days, it seems, we can barely touch a child without fear of arrest, but 60 summers ago the world was a simpler place. Guards and ticket collectors were kindly men, and expert in removing grit with the aid of a pocket handkerchief carried specifically for the purpose, their first aid being invariably accompanied by a stern warning "never again" to lean out.

At last, as the afternoon shadows began to lengthen, we covered those final, familiar miles. Past fields of buttercups and grazing cattle, past little streams running between banks of red earth. Past Colebrooke church perched on its well-remembered hill-top, and with much huffing and puffing up the gradient to Copplestone, the highest point along the branch line.

And so, finally, to Morchard Road. A diminutive child of six or seven clutching his brown "Revelation" suitcase opens the door and climbs down, as often as not the only alighting passenger. And there she would be, a slight bespectacled figure in her late sixties. As always, she would be wearing a sober navy blue -- her favourite colour; blue skirt, blue pullover with the amber brooch, blue jacket, blue handbag and navy blue leather gloves. Her grey hair, immaculately secured in its hairnet, drawn back in a bun and pinned carefully to the wide brimmed hat of dark blue straw that she invariably wore for driving. A frail lavender-scented spinster come to meet the London child she loved, and to rejoice with him in the beginning of another summer.

STRIKING OUT ON YOUR OWN?

Footpaths and bridleways are clearly marked on the Ordnance Survey's Explorer Series (1:25,000 scale) maps. The following sheets are especially relevant:

    113 Okehampton
    114 Exeter & the Exe Valley
    127 South Molton & Chulmleigh
    139 Bideford, Ilfracombe & Barnstaple

ANY COMMENTS?

The author (and Scrumpy) would appreciate learning of any inaccuracies or receiving any other comments via e-mail: pcbcraske@gmail.com

LESS STRAIN ON YOUR PURSE

Since it first saw the light of day in 2009, *Tarka Line Walks* has attracted sponsors willing to underwrite the project. Their generous support for this book means that its RRP can be kept below £10 -- less than 17p per walk. The author and publisher encourage you to support the book's sponsors, whose advertisements have done much to protect your pocket!

COPYRIGHT

Tarka Line Walks

This first edition published in 2013 by Crimson Publishing Ltd., Westminster House, Kew Road, Richmond, Surrey TW9 2ND

www.crimsonpublishing.co.uk
© Crimson Publishing 2013

TEXT & PHOTOGRAPHS © Peter C.B. Craske (unless otherwise stated). The right of Peter C.B. Craske to be identified as the author of this work has been asserted by him in accordance with the Copyright, Designs and Patents Act 1988.

MAPS This product includes mapping data licensed from Ordnance Survey® with the permission of the Controller of Her Majesty's Stationery Office. © Crown Copyright 2013. All rights reserved. Licence number 150002047. Ordnance Survey and the OS symbol are registered trademarks and Explorer, Landranger and Outdoor Leisure are trademarks of the Ordnance Survey, the national mapping agency of Great Britain.

VINTAGE PUBLICITY © Science & Society Picture Library; Southern Posters (pp.46 & 84)

SKETCHES Brian Siggery © Tarka Rail Assoc.

British Library Cataloguing in Publication Data

A catalogue record for this book is available from the British Library

ISBN 978 1 78059 1827

Graphic design Touchwood Design, Okehampton EX20 1DY

Printed and bound in the UK by Ashford Colour Press, Gosport, Hants